TORONTO

100 YEARS OF GRANDEUR

The front door of Beverley House. The house itself was demolished long ago, but one can still walk through its front door through which Toronto's pillars of society and government once came and went. The door is on display today at the Royal Ontario Museum.
— The Globe and Mail

TORONTO

100 YEARS OF GRANDEUR

THE INSIDE STORIES OF TORONTO'S GREAT HOMES
AND THE PEOPLE WHO LIVED THERE

LUCY BOOTH MARTYN

**PAGURIAN
PRESS**

Copyright ©1978, 1984 The Pagurian Corporation Limited
13 Hazelton Avenue, Toronto, Canada

Copyright under the Berne Convention. All rights reserved. No part
of this book may be reproduced in any form without the permission
of the publishers.

ISBN 0-88932-118-3
Printed and bound in Canada

Contents

For my mother,
Nellie Reid,
who encouraged me

Introduction

The name "Toronto" has appeared on early maps since 1673. With various spellings, it has been assigned to forts, lakes, bays, rivers, and tracts of land between Lakes Ontario and Simcoe. Its meaning, derived from Indian names, has had several plausible interpretations, but the one most usually accepted is "place of meeting."

Various Indian tribes met at the mouth of the Toronto River (now the Humber) to trade with each other and with Dutch, French, and English traders. The settlement there was the southern terminus of an important trail, the shortest and easiest route from Lake Ontario to the Holland River and upper lakes.

The "Toronto Purchase" was first discussed with the Mississauga Indians in September 1787 by Deputy Surveyor General John Collins, representing Lord Dorchester, the Governor General, at the Carrying Place, Bay of Quinte. The King's representative held a small orb in his hand to indicate his authority, and there was an ornate bag on the table to represent the Privy Purse. In a similar ceremony, one Indian chief carried a string of wampum and another held a flat stone marked with a cross to signify a boundary. The Crown bought more than 250,000 acres of land for £1,700 and goods, which included 149 barrels of cloth, brass kettles, blankets, mirrors, laced hats, tobacco, guns, powder, and flints, rum, and ninety-six other items.

When Upper Canada was made a separate province in 1791, Colonel John Graves Simcoe became its first Lieutenant Governor. He disliked

Indian geographical names, which he considered "outlandish," and changed the names of rivers, lakes, and settlements to more familiar English names. He changed the name of his first capital from Niagara to Newark, and the Toronto River became the Humber River.

Simcoe decided to build his new town not at the mouth of the Humber where there was a small settlement, but about five miles eastward near the mouth of a river the Indians called Nichingquakokonik. We can forgive Simcoe for changing this name — he called the river the Don — and when he established his capital at Toronto he changed that euphonious name to York. On August 27, 1793, to the roll of drums and the boom of a twenty-one-gun Royal Salute fired by the troops and answered by the ships in the Bay, the new town was christened York (alias "Muddy Little York" for the next forty years) in honour of the glorious victories of the King's son, Frederick, Duke of York. Simcoe wished to please the King, and it is to be hoped that poor, sick George III was having one of his good days when the momentous news reached him.

Simcoe intended York to be only a temporary capital. It had a fine harbour, and would be an excellent naval base until he could establish the permanent capital on the Thames River, in the heart of the province (now London), which he had decided would be a safer location.

Meanwhile Lord Dorchester, the Governor General, had his own plans for the seat of government of Upper Canada. He intended to make Kingston the capital. But the infant York confounded both Lieutenant Governor and Governor General. It remained the capital and eventually reverted to its Indian name of Toronto.

From the beginning York enjoyed thoughtful town planning. It was never a village, but was, in Simcoe's words, "our Royal Town of York." It did not grow gradually from a straggling hamlet beside a millpond, as so many towns did, but was created by an act of government and began life as a sturdy adolescent. It was the provincial capital, a garrison town — an important centre. Although small — only ten blocks at first — Simcoe and his advisers planned it carefully on paper before a single building was erected.

All street lines of the early plans were straight and intersected sharply at right angles. Toronto has fewer winding streets than most cities, although there are several which follow old Indian trails, taking the shortest route between two points and detouring only for serious obstacles, but early York's surveys were like the Roman roads — they disregarded forests, rivers, hills, ravines, and swamps. In attempting to conform to this rigid grid pattern, early streets were often compelled to end abruptly when a physical obstacle was encountered. The street continued farther on. Streets frequently had to wait many years before finances and engineering ability improved sufficiently to build bridges over ravines or rivers, grade hills, or drain swamps so that a street might be continued in its undeviating straight line.

The first ten-block site of thirty acres was a parallelogram bounded on the west by George Street, on the north by Duchess Street (which later became Duke Street, and is now part of Adelaide Street), on the east by Berkeley Street (now Parliament Street), and on the south by King Street (later Palace and now Front Street). Land eastward to the Don River, known as The Common, was reserved for government use, and land on the west end to the Humber River was reserved for military use.

Officials were given one-acre town lots, and regulations were laid down by Simcoe and his Council for the houses to be built thereon. Those on the front streets must be set back at least twelve feet from the street, be of two storeys in height, at least forty-seven feet wide, and of an approved, uniform style of architecture. Houses on the second streets might be somewhat smaller, but must still be of two storeys and an approved style, while builders in back streets were allowed more freedom to build according to their circumstances. As one correspondent reported to a friend in October 1793, ". . . seriously, our good Governor is a little wild in his projects. . . ."

As was to be expected, the early restrictions were not always observed.

When Simcoe left in 1796, not many of his fine plans had been carried out, and it was the Honourable Peter Russell who laid the practical foundations of York. He immediately extended the western boundary to York Street and then to Peter Street, and the northern boundary to Lot Street (now Queen Street). Space was allotted for a school, church, hospital, and jail.

Beyond the town plot, the township, also called York, was divided into square blocks of one and a quarter miles each way, containing one thousand acres each. From present Queen to Bloor Streets, each block contained ten lots of one hundred acres each, although there were no roads bounding the blocks. The lots were long, narrow strips, ten chains wide (or forty rods or one-eighth of a mile, or six hundred and sixty feet). Their depth, of one hundred chains, was a mile and a quarter. These were "park" lots given to officials and prominent Loyalists to compensate for the expense of moving from the first capital at Newark, and to enable them to preserve the dignity of their position. Restrictions prohibited partition of the park lots.

North of Bloor Street, the one-thousand-acre blocks contained five two-hundred-acre lots, being one-quarter of a mile wide and a mile and a quarter deep. The boundaries of the blocks were known as "concession" lines. The first concession from the Bay was Lot Street, with a broken concession between it and the lake. Bloor Street was the second concession from the Bay, and St. Clair Avenue the third.

When York was incorporated as the City of Toronto in 1834, its boundaries were Bathurst Street on the west, Parliament Street on the east, Lake Ontario on the south, and a line twelve hundred feet north of Queen Street (approximately modern Dundas Street) on the north. The area between these boundaries and Dufferin, Bloor, and the Don River was known as the "liberties." All restrictions on speculative development were removed.

By 1850 the city limits had become Bloor Street on the north, Dufferin Street on the west, and the Don River on the east, and in the 1880s Toronto began greedily swallowing its suburban villages. In 1883 Yorkville was annexed, Brockton and Riverdale in 1884, Rosedale and The Annex in 1887, Seaton Village and Sunnyside in 1888, Parkdale in 1889, North Rosedale in 1906, Deer Park and East Toronto in 1908, Wychwood, Bracondale, West Toronto, and Balmy Beach in 1909, Earlscourt and Dovercourt in 1910, and North Toronto and Moore Park in 1912. This rapid expansion of acreage and population stretched the resources of the city to the utmost, and there followed a quiet period while the new territory was digested. When the annexations were consolidated, Toronto was ready for further expansion.

Since its founding, York-Toronto has had many colourful citizens, who have dwelt in a great variety of houses. Early settlers tried, when circumstances permitted, to build their new homes similar to fondly remembered homes across the sea, and it was natural to give the name of the old house where they had been born to the new one in the wilderness. This eased the loneliness of the first years, and gave a reassuring sense of continuity to their lives. Sometimes nostalgia led to naming the new house for the village or shire from which a family had emigrated, but often a simple name, descriptive of its surroundings, was given to the new home.

In a day when street numbers were unknown and even streets not yet opened beyond the small core of the town, it was essential for houses to have names, either historic or merely descriptive, such as The Oaks or Riverview. When a child or a dog or a horse receives a name, that child or animal becomes an individual, and when a house is given a name, it acquires an identity and a personality. The houses described in the following chapters were not always those of the most prominent citizens, nor were they necessarily the largest or the most distinguished architecturally, but they all possessed personality, and they all had names.

Once a man's residence was given a name, the whole estate was known henceforth by that name. Deeds of property, wills, advertisements for sale, all referred to the property by its name. A family became identified with the name of its home. Correspondence and society news invariably referred to a family by the name of its property, sometimes even omitting the family name. Friends wrote, for example, that they had visited Glen Edyth or Spadina. It was not necessary to mention that they had been visiting the Nordheimers or the Baldwins. Frequently the name of the property was used to identify a branch of a large family. One spoke of the Mashquoteh Baldwins, to distinguish them from the Spadina Baldwins, or the Rusholme Denisons as distinct from the Dover Court Denisons. Sometimes a family was known by the name of their home.

In many cases a section of Toronto became known by the name of an early house, for example, Rosedale, Deer Park, Wychwood, Sunnyside. A great many Toronto streets bear the names of historic private homes.

The houses are described in all their architectural diversity, from the harmonious symmetry of the Georgian homes built by the early Establishment (*Beverley House*), through whimsical Regency cottages (*Colborne Lodge*), to the picturesque Gothic Revival style (*Oaklands*). Some were in the Italianate Villa style, as *Sherborne Villa*, although it was minus the usual watchtower; many on Beverley Street were in the Second Empire style with mansard roofs, and, finally, there were the Victorian mansions with their flamboyant individuality.

The careers of the men who built and occupied these houses are outlined as they developed and moulded their city. Their lives and their homes illustrate Toronto's history and reflect the changing tastes of each generation.

Unfortunately, many of the houses have been demolished. A number have survived, shorn of their verandahs and spacious grounds. *Drumsnab* and *Wychwood* are still private residences. *Chudleigh* on Beverley Street, home of George Beardmore, is now the COSTI Italian Education Centre. John Howard's *Colborne Lodge* is a museum and John Ross Robertson's *Culloden* on Sherbourne Street is a Training Centre for the Ontario Provincial Police. *Devon House*, John Cawthra's home on Beverley Street, is headquarters for Jewish Social Services. Hart Massey's *Euclid Hall* is a restaurant, and Edgar Jarvis's *Glen Hurst* is part of Branksome Hall School.

George Brown's *Lambton Lodge* is a school for Metro Toronto's retarded children, Sir Oliver Mowat's *Northfield* houses the executive offices of the Toronto branch of the Canadian Broadcasting Corporation, William Thomas's *Oakham House* is now the Student Union of Ryerson Polytechnic Institute, and Senator John Macdonald's *Oaklands* is part of De La Salle College. Frederick Cumberland's *Pendarvis* on St. George Street is the International Student Centre at the University of Toronto.

These historic mansions, now restored and modernized, have had checkered careers. We can still walk through them and see how Toronto's influential families once lived. They are our visual heritage.

Toronto: 100 Years of Grandeur covers the first century of Toronto's history.

The Canvas House
1791

The first Government House in Toronto was a tent, a most unusual tent. It was never called a tent, however, but "The Canvas House."

When Colonel John Graves Simcoe left England in September 1791 to become the first Lieutenant Governor of Upper Canada, he took with him a number of tents of various sizes and shapes. He had bought several at an auction sale of the property of Captain James Cook, the celebrated explorer. Captain Cook and Captain John Simcoe, father of Governor Simcoe, had been friends and fellow officers in the Royal Navy. (Later, when Simcoe named a lake in Upper Canada after his father, he named a bay in that lake for Captain Cook.)

The tents had been especially constructed as a mobile home, which Cook had occupied in various tropical islands more than twenty years before. Simcoe saw them and thought they would be useful in a land where there were as yet few permanent buildings. After examining the Cook tents, Simcoe ordered two more to be built with several improved features. These are described in accounts rendered in March and April 1792 for "Two Canvas Rooms made in frames, each 38'4" long × 12' wide and 7'2" high at the sides, with 6 glazed windows and a partition to each room, also a cosy iron stove, fender, shovel, poker and tongs, the inside of the rooms papered complete, the outside painted in oil colour and properly packed, marked and numbered, included at per room £100 − £200." There was also an invoice for camp tables and chairs "packed with the canvas houses."

Simcoe set up a temporary capital at Newark at the mouth of the Niagara River, where he occupied Navy Hall. Although they did not live in the Canvas House at Niagara, Mrs. Simcoe found it useful on one occasion. In February 1793 she wrote to Mrs. Hunt who was caring for her four older daughters at Wolford, Devonshire: "There are many balls. . . . I have not attended them because I was the greatest part of the winter in daily expectation of being confined. I have taken the canvas house we brought from England for my own apartment; it makes two very comfortable and remarkably warm private rooms; it is boarded outside to prevent snow lying on it. The comfort I derived from these apartments was extremely great when I lay in, because being in a manner separate from the rest of the house, it was so very quiet. . . ." The reference is to the birth of her daughter Katherine on January 16th, not mentioned in her diary.

Simcoe first visited Toronto in May 1793, and in July Mrs. Simcoe and the three young children — Sophia, not quite four years old, Francis aged two, and the baby — and their nurse sailed across the lake from Niagara to Toronto. They lived in the Canvas House and Colonel Simcoe joined them a week later. According to her diary, the Canvas House was erected "on a rising ground divided by a creek from the camp which is ordered to be cleared immediately." This would be about where the Old Fort is today, near the foot of Bathurst Street and, at that time, quite close to the lake.

At this time Mrs. Simcoe wrote, "The partition was put in the Canvas House today, by which means I have a bedroom in it, as well as a sitting room. The rooms are very comfortable, about 30 feet long."

There were no parliament buildings, and, as a result, the Canvas House became not only the vice-royal residence, but served as the first official Government Building. Colonel Simcoe held his first reception there, and the Executive Council met there for its first meeting in Toronto. Official dinners, assemblies, and even balls were held in it; private soldiers from the Queen's Rangers acted as servants. The Canvas House was the social centre of the province. A flag flew from a tall staff before the entrance, and soldiers were always on sentry duty.

The Canvas House had wooden doors and was partitioned into public and private quarters. It had vertical sides to a good height, which

Colonel John Graves Simcoe (1752-1806), first Governor of Upper Canada, and the lively Mrs. Simcoe in Welsh dress. — Ontario Archives

then sloped up to the ridge. Being covered with oil, the canvas was quite waterproof. The floors were of plank, built in sections and held together by screws in such a way that the whole could be quickly dismantled, transported to a new location, and then reassembled by the soldiers. A tent with glass windows and several rooms was such a novelty that it provided endless conversation for those who viewed it for the first time.

Mrs. Simcoe always welcomed new adventures and we gather from her cheerful comments in the famous diary that she enjoyed her unconventional accommodation. Some of her contemporaries, however, were shocked. Peter Russell, the Receiver General, wrote to his sister Elizabeth back in Newark, ". . . the Governor and Mrs. Simcoe received me graciously, but you can have no conception of the misery in which they live. The Canvas House being their only residence — in one room of which they lie and see company — and in the other are the nurse and children squalling etc."

"The canvas house we use as a bedroom, but the other is going to be erected for a winter dining room," Mrs. Simcoe wrote in September 1794. The winter of 1793-94 was spent at Toronto, which Simcoe had renamed York, and for the cold months the Canvas House was boarded up on the outside and banked with earth. With rugs on the plank floors and a good fire in the stove, the house became quite comfortable, probably more so than the tents and log huts occupied by the soldiers and early settlers. According to one observer, "Frail as was its substance, it was rendered exceedingly comfortable, and soon became as distinguished for its urbane hospitality as for the peculiarity of its structure."

The Canvas House migrated a number of times along the lakeshore. Doubtless this seemed an advantage to Mrs. Simcoe, who enjoyed a change of scene. At one time it was near the old French fort (near the present Dufferin Street), at another time it stood as far east as the modern Gooderham distillery.

Even Mrs. William Jarvis, wife of the Provincial Secretary, who usually had a sharp tongue and an even sharper pen, admitted that the canvas houses were quite superior. Writing from Newark in September 1793 to her father in England, "The Governor and family are gone to Toronto (now York) where it is said they winter. The Governor has two canvas houses. Everybody are [sic] sick at York, but no matter, the Lady likes the place, therefore everyone else must. When you come, bring with you a Canvas House, it will save you many a pound and cold fingers. It can be boarded up and serve for a good warm house."

March 1794 was bitterly cold. For the first time Mrs. Simcoe admitted discomfort in the Canvas House. "Tho' I wore 3 fur tippets I was so cold I could hardly hold my cards this evening — this is the first time we have felt the want of a ceiling which we have not had made in our drawing room because the room was rather low. . . ." The next day, the fifth of March, "Very cold, I divided the room by hanging across it a large carpet which made it warmer."

After Governor Simcoe departed from Canada in 1796, the Canvas House still remained an important social centre. "The officers of the Queen's Rangers request the honour of Mr. and Mrs. Ridout's company to a Ball on Friday evening next, at the Canvas Houses," according to an invitation dated December 11, 1799.

Castle Frank

1793 - 1829

The desire for a rustic retreat is shared by great and humble alike. Castle Frank was the first summer cottage built by a Toronto family. It was a log house, unusual in several respects, and, because its entrance was in the narrow end where there was a portico, it resembled a Greek temple. Four unpeeled logs acted as columns supporting the projecting roof of the gable and the pediment thus formed lent it a classical air.

Elizabeth Posthuma Gwillim was born in Whitchurch, England, on the border of Wales. Her father, Lt. Col. Thomas Gwillim, aide-de-campe to General Wolfe, fought at the capture of Quebec in 1759. He died in 1766, seven months before the birth of Elizabeth. Her mother died at her birth. The orphan was an heiress, reared by her mother's sister, wife of Admiral Samuel Graves, whose godson was Colonel John Graves Simcoe, commander of the celebrated Queen's Rangers during the American Revolutionary War. When Elizabeth was sixteen Simcoe visited his godparents, and he and Elizabeth fell in love. In 1782 they were married.

Mrs. Simcoe's money bought the Wolford estate in Devonshire and built a splendid new house there, to which they moved in 1786. Simcoe was elected to Parliament and Wolford became the centre of much gaiety. Life as landed gentry ended in 1791 when Colonel Simcoe was appointed Lieutenant Governor of the new province of Upper Canada.

Castle Frank from a drawing by Mrs. Simcoe made on birch bark, probably in 1794.
— Ontario Archives

Mrs. Simcoe was then twenty-five years old, five feet tall, fluent in French and German, could read and write Spanish, loved dancing and riding, and had a genuine talent for sketching. She was also the mother of Eliza, Charlotte, Henrietta, Caroline, Sophia, and one son, Francis Gwillim.

Leaving the four older girls at Wolford in the care of an old friend, the Simcoes took Sophia, not quite two years old, and Francis, aged three months, with them. Simcoe took the oath of office at Kingston in July 1792, then moved on to Niagara where a temporary capital was established and the name changed to Newark.

Mrs. Simcoe kept a detailed diary illustrated with graphic sketches. Her maps and drawings are very accurate and are our only record of many early scenes. The diary mentions unusual plants and insects, describes Indians, rattlesnakes, and scenery — but makes no mention of the birth of her daughter Katherine at Niagara in January 1793.

When Mrs. Simcoe went to Toronto in July she had with her three small children, and, although accommodation was primitive, she was cheerful and vivacious. Early in August they rowed eastward along the lakeshore to the "highlands of Toronto . . . the shore is extremely bold and has the appearance of Chalk Cliffs. They appeared so well that we talked of building a summer residence there and calling it Scarborough."

Governor Simcoe expected the town to develop around the mouth of the Don River. With his wife, officers, and ladies, he frequently rode to the Don, and took boat trips up the river. Simcoe decided to build a summer retreat on the high bank of the Don where they could relax far from the pomp of vice-regal life, and, according to the entry on October 29, 1973,

> The Governor having determined to take a lot of 200 acres upon the River Don for Francis and the law obliges persons having lots of land to build a house upon them within a year, we went today to fix upon the spot for building the house. We went six miles by water from the Fort and east along the bay shore to the Don, and up that river, landed, climbed up an exceedingly steep hill, or rather a series of sugar-loafed hills, and approved of the highest spot from whence we looked down on the tops of large trees. There are large pine plains around it which being without underwood I can ride and walk on, and we hope the height will secure us from mosquitoes. We dined by a large fire on wild ducks and chowder on the side of a hill opposite to that spot.

Building soon began on the lot patented in the name of Francis Simcoe, and the property was given the whimsical name of "Castle Frank." The site, high on a narrow plateau above the steep west bank of the winding river, was wild and picturesque. It was covered with magnificent pine, elm, and butternut trees. The house was just north of the present boundary of St. James' Cemetery and south of modern Bloor Street East.

Castle Frank differed from the usual log cabin. It was probably the only one in the province using the French manner of cornering. Tight fitting corners are essential in a log house, since water collects when spaces are left and rots the wood. British and American builders had various ways of notching, keying, or dovetailing logs, but the French used the mortise and tenon method. Short horizontal logs with protruding tenons fitted into slots in vertical posts at the corners and at intervals along the walls. Vertical logs also supported window frames. Since the French usually covered the logs with protective sheathing, Castle Frank's squared logs were neatly clapboarded.

Castle Frank was fifty feet long, thirty feet wide, sixteen feet high at the eaves, and four feet higher in the centre. It faced south, the doors were in the ends with a portico front and back. There were four windows on each side, with sixteen small panes in each, covered by shutters of double thickness, made of planks horizontal on one side and vertical on the other, studded with large nails. The doors were similar. A massive chimney of several flues rose from the centre of the roof.

The interior was divided into two rooms, each with a fireplace. The Simcoes began brief excursions to Castle Frank after New Year's 1794, and although it was unfinished, they were so charmed they occasionally stayed overnight or for weekends. A bridle path was made along the riverbank and up a long slope to the plateau. Soldiers cut a narrow carriage road through the woods from York, which appears on an early map as Park Lane. Today's Parliament Street in part follows this road.

The river Don was then clear and deep, and Mrs. Simcoe enjoyed watching the Indians spearing salmon in its swift waters. Seated in a carriole, she too tried ice-fishing.

The spring of 1794 was a sad time. Baby Katherine died in April and for several weeks the heartbroken mother left her diary blank. She spent some months at Newark and Quebec while the Governor toured the province. The following summer they were back at York. On June 1st she wrote, "I went in a boat to Francis's estate" and on the 6th, "Francis gave a dinner on his birthday to the soldiers' children." (This may have been in the Canvas House; the diary is not specific.)

Castle Frank was still not finished. "We walked on the ice to the house which is building on Francis's land," she wrote in January 1796, and the next month she took a group of ladies to Castle Frank. "The ice was not so good, and the snow melted. It was so mild that we could not wear greatcoats. Francis has a small sleigh which the servants have taught a goat to draw; he is the handsomest goat I ever saw."

Frequent excursions were made on the ice of the Don. It was much pleasanter to skim over the frozen surface in a carriole than to follow the rough, muddy path at other seasons. In April she wrote, "Francis has not been well. We therefore set off for Castle Frank today to change the air, intending to pass some days there — the house being yet unfinished we divided the large room by sail-cloth — pitched the tent in the inner part, and slept on wooden beds. The Porticos here are delightfully pleasant and the room cool from its height and the thickness of the logs. Francis is much better and busy planting currant bushes and Peach trees."

"Sent the children to Castle Frank in a boat," she wrote on June 30, "We rode there thro' those pleasant shady Pine Plains now covered with sweet scented fern."

Castle Frank had a basement. On July 7, according to the diary, "The weather excessively hot and we find the underground room very comfortable, the windows on one side are cut through the side of the hill." A few days later, "Rode to dine at Castle Frank, so heavy a shower of rain that we were obliged to quit the lower room, the windows of which are not glazed — slept there."

Simcoe, now Major General, was about to return to England. "Took leave of Castle Frank," she wrote on July 20. In 1806 Simcoe died, just as he was preparing to go to India as Commander-in-Chief, leaving his widow with nine children. Francis was not destined to return to York to enjoy his two hundred acres at Castle Frank. He was killed in Spain in 1812 — a twenty-year-old lieutenant.

Mrs. Simcoe survived her husband by forty-four years, frequently referring to "that pretty spot Castle Frank." She made a number of sketches of it from different angles; the best one was drawn on birch bark.

She refused to permit any of her seven daughters to marry; they did not even dare to sit in her presence without permission. The girls inherited her artistic talents and embellished the Wolford Chapel with their carving in wood and stone. They also made stained glass and when Mrs. Simcoe's friend, Mrs. Susan Sibbald, built a wooden church beside her home Eildon Hall near Jackson's Point on Lake Simcoe, a stained glass window designed and executed by her daughters was presented by Mrs. Simcoe in 1845. This window with its seven crosses representing the girls was later moved to the new stone church at Sibbald Point.

Only after Mrs. Simcoe died did one daughter, Anne, then about fifty years old, venture to marry.

In 1966 Ontario accepted the gift of Wolford Chapel in whose tiny graveyard are buried the province's first Lieutenant Governor, his wife, and several members of his family.

Meanwhile, Castle Frank was used by Peter Russell who administered the province. Picnics and balls continued to be held there, but the only family ever to occupy it was that of John Denison, Russell's friend. They lived there for several months.

In 1803 his former secretary, Colonel Talbot, wrote General Simcoe, ''I paid a visit to Castle Frank which I am sorry to add is uninhabited and going to ruin. Some rascals have broken off the window shutters and gone down to the lower apartment where they broke down the chimney in order to carry away the bar of iron which supported it.''

In the summer of 1813 when the Americans returned to York, they sent a boat up the Don to investigate a story they had heard of the ''Governor's Castle.'' What a disappointment to find only a ruined log house!

In 1829 transient fishermen set fire to Castle Frank. Some planks and flooring were salvaged by John Scadding, Simcoe's Devonshire manager, who built a lean-to on his house on the east side of the Don near the present Gerrard Street.

Much of the Castle Frank lot became part of St. James' Cemetery. Years later a new Castle Frank was built by Sir Edward Kemp north of the original house, but it was demolished before Castle Frank High School was built. The school stands close to the site of the Simcoes' sylvan retreat and Castle Frank Crescent now runs through the property.

Berkeley House
1794-1925

Berkeley House was the first house built in York, and it was near the southwest corner of the present King Street East and Berkeley Street that George Porter, a former militia sergeant, built himself a crude little cabin of hewn logs in 1794. He used it as a fishing hut. Although a great house was eventually built around it, the logs and the little cabin remained at the core.

Among the officials who accompanied Governor Simcoe to Canada in 1791 was one Major John Small, the first clerk of the Executive Council and Clerk of the Crown. Although Newark was the seat of the new government and most officials were building homes there, Major Small bought the little log house from Porter in 1795 for fifty dollars — on condition that Porter shingle the roof. Small then greatly enlarged the primitive structure with squared white pine logs sixty feet long, and one-and-a-half-inch-thick floors. The house, however, remained one storey high.

Small had been born in 1746 in Gloucestershire, England, near the market town of Berkeley, which was famous for its ancient castle. Colonel Berkeley, the owner of Berkeley Castle, and Major Small were close friends, and Major Small decided to call his new home "Berkeley House" in honour of his friend.

Several years later York was surveyed and a block reserved for future government buildings. It was found that Berkeley House, on its one-acre lot, stood on a corner of the square intended by Simcoe for

Government House. Porter, however, had received the lot from the surveyor, Alexander Aitkin, and Major Small was allowed to stay, although only after some anxious delay.

While the Parliament Buildings were being built the Executive Council frequently met in Berkeley House. They sat around the huge dining table, and Major Small, as Clerk, recorded the minutes. He was a man of boundless hospitality, well known for keeping open house. He liked to stand at his front door in his knee breeches, silk stockings, and silver-buckled shoes, inviting passing friends and acquaintances to come in for dinner. Governor Simcoe and other officials were frequent guests.

On September 4, 1793, park lots of one hundred acres, from modern Queen Street north to Bloor Street, were granted to government officials. They numbered westward from the Don to the Humber River, and number three, from Sumach to Sackville Street, was assigned to John Small. The neighbouring lot, number four, from Sackville to Parliament Street, was granted to his friend John White, the first Attorney General.

On one occasion, Mrs. Small and Mrs. John Elmsley, the wife of the Chief Justice, cut Mrs. White. In the tiny new town, society was ingrown and there were few diversions. Petty differences were magnified out of all proportion. Mrs. White told her husband how Mrs. Small had insulted her, and he, in poor health and with an irritable disposition, became wildly indignant. During the 1799 Christmas festivities while wine flowed freely, he told some slanderous stories about Mrs. Small to David Smith, the Surveyor General. Smith was indiscreet enough to repeat the stories to John Elmsley and to others. The gossip spread until the whole town was involved. When Major Small heard the stories, he felt compelled to challenge White to a duel.

On January 3, 1800, in a grove behind the Parliament Buildings, a pistol duel was held. John White was mortally wounded and, after thirty-six hours of agony, died. Before he died he asked that his body be wrapped in a sheet and buried in his garden.

Major Small was tried for murder. The jury, following the custom of the day, acquitted him. Mrs. Small's reputation, however, was ruined, and for many years most of the ladies of York snubbed her. Society in

Major John Small, the first Clerk of the Executive Council and Clerk of the Crown, and Mrs. Small — the cause of the famous duel which mortally wounded John White. Major Small was tried for murder but was acquitted.

— Metropolitan Toronto Library Board

the little capital took sides in the matter, and there was much bitterness. Poor Mrs. White and her three children returned to England to live in genteel poverty. John Small lived until 1831.

His son, Charles Coxwell Small, inherited Berkeley House, having also taken over as Clerk of the Crown and Pleas in 1825 when his father resigned. Charles Small was Colonel of the 4th York Militia for many years. In 1849 he completely rebuilt Berkeley House. He elevated the original section and added a large gabled wing on each side, parallel to it. The three wings were connected by another large wing across the back which extended farther east than the front section. This wing had large bay windows on the ground floor. The new building was two storeys high, with walls of hand-made, eighteen-inch-thick brick, covered by stucco. The upper windows were Gothic and fitted with shutters. The windows of the original section were changed and given round heads to match those in the new wings. The result was a large, rambling house with a somewhat quaint but stately appearance. Its

Berkeley House in the 1840s — an E-shaped English manor house, somewhat quaint, but stately.

— Metropolitan Toronto Library Board

style was reminiscent of English manor houses built in the shape of a huge E to flatter the first Queen Elizabeth.

There were thirteen large rooms, but the drawing room and dining room in the west wing were especially grand. Each was forty-five feet long and eighteen feet wide. The beautiful rosewood table in the dining room could comfortably seat twenty guests, and frequently it did. A rosewood sideboard, equally massive, with lead-lined wine cellaret, was covered with large silver dishes. Oil portraits of Major Small and his wife Eliza hung on the wall above the sideboard. The walls were covered with pictures, but, in the custom of the day, great lengths of wire were frankly visible. On the wall opposite the sideboard was a marble mantelpiece above an arched fireplace.

Charles died in 1864, and his son John, Taxing Master, Collector of

Berkeley House in 1925 just before it was demolished — a pathetic ruin.
— Metropolitan Toronto Library Board

Customs for the Port of Toronto, and Member of the Legislature, became the new owner. In 1874 the house was altered once again. The original logs in the central wing were still in perfect condition, and crowds collected to see the last of the great squared timbers being hauled away.

In 1909 John Small died. Three years later his widow, Susan, sold Berkeley House. The character of King Street East had altered; there were now rows of stores where once there had been only fine mansions and beautiful lawns.

The big house was divided into three separate houses, each of a good size, but it was difficult to keep them occupied. After 1916 they stood vacant. Finally, in 1925, the venerable landmark was demolished, and a factory was built on the site.

Russell Abbey

1797-1856

"He's called the Receiver-General because he's generally receiving!"

"He would grant land to the devil himself and all his family, as good Loyalists, if he could only collect the patent fees!"

These and similar unkind remarks about the Honourable Peter Russell were freely circulated in the early days of York, usually by men jealous of his position. It has been the custom to condemn Russell for greediness and to ridicule his ambitions, completely ignoring the conditions of the day and the achievements of his administration.

It is true that Peter Russell did acquire large holdings of land, but so did other early officials. As Executive Councillor, he was entitled to 6,000 acres and there were, in addition, other grants because of his other offices. All early officials were given large land grants to uphold the dignity of their office. United Empire Loyalists were granted 1,200 acres and their wives and children were each granted the same amount. Alexander Grant, for example, was given 18,000 acres, W.D. Powell 15,600 acres, and Aeneas Shaw 19,200 acres.

Bachelor Russell must have had bitter thoughts concerning an authority which appeared to gauge a man's loyalty by the size of his family. Peter was scrupulously honest; it has never been suggested that he obtained any land by dishonest means. His office did, however, give Russell inside information which enabled him to choose the best land available in the most convenient location.

Russell Abbey was the home of the Honourable Peter Russell and his sister Elizabeth. Like most eighteenth century York houses it was only one storey high. At the time it was considered commodious and dignified, even elegant.

— Metropolitan Toronto Library Board

Peter Russell was born in 1733 in Cork, Ireland, the son of Richard Russell, an impecunious captain in the army but well connected with the English Russells, whose head was the Duke of Bedford. The Irish branch of the family were small landowners, Anglican and Tory, whose males usually went into either the Church or the Army.

After a short period at Cambridge, where he pursued pleasure more than study, Peter secured an army commission. He saw duty at Gibraltar and along the Barbary Coast, and was then sent to North America to serve under General Braddock. Eventually he was forced to sell his commission to pay his mountainous gambling debts and spent a quiet interval supervising an estate in North Carolina. In 1771 he returned to England in hopes of obtaining a suitable civil appointment. When this failed Peter began the study of physic. Two years later his gambling debts had again grown to such heights he had to flee to Rotterdam to escape imprisonment. The following year a Bill was passed for the Relief of Insolvent Debtors, and Peter returned to England.

Unable to obtain a lucrative civil position, he again went into the army in 1776, in time to take part in the American campaign. Peter was appointed assistant secretary to Sir Henry Clinton, Commander--in-Chief of the British forces. His fortunes began to improve. He became a captain in the 64th Regiment, a judge of the Court of Vice-Admiralty of South Carolina, and Superintendent of the Port of Charleston. But Charleston surrendered and his fine position evaporated before he could assume his duties.

He returned to England with Sir Henry Clinton in 1782 and helped Clinton write his history of the American war, all the while seeking a good position. It was an age when appointments were seldom made on merit alone. Patronage was rife and a man could write dozens of letters to influential men and wait for years, hoping desperately that someone would act on his behalf. Peter Russell was heavily in debt as usual, partly because he had assumed responsibility for the support of his improvident father and for his spinster half-sister Elizabeth. She was seventeen years younger than Peter, but she and Peter were devoted to each other, corresponding at great length whenever he was absent.

In 1790 Peter met Colonel John Graves Simcoe at Clinton's house. Simcoe suggested that he recommend Peter to go to Upper Canada as Receiver General and Auditor. Peter hesitated, still hoping for something good in England. His last hopes were soon dashed, so he accepted the post which Clinton helped him secure. Simcoe explained that although the salary was modest, there would be compensation in large land grants.

On August 15, 1791, Peter wrote Elizabeth, "It will certainly be a very handsomely gilded pill, though an unpleasant one," and he spoke of the various officials going out. Three weeks later he wrote again, "Mr. Pitt has consented to appoint me Receiver General of Upper Canada, accompanied with a seat on both Councils and a salary of £300 per annum, without deductions." He added that he still hoped to exchange this for some post at home. In December 1791 his friend Captain John Smith wrote to Peter, commiserating with him on his "cursed American banishment."

He sailed in March 1792 almost against his will, hoping to make a quick fortune and return to England. Elizabeth accompanied him. Russell was then fifty-nine years old. His portrait shows a stout man with heavy eyes, a large, straight nose, and a cleft chin.

The post of Receiver General was the equivalent of the modern Provincial Treasurer and Auditor. The salary appeared adequate with opportunities for additional perquisites. Russell soon found that part of his salary was in land (which could hardly be given away, since there were such generous free grants) and in fees on land patents, which were often extremely slow in being paid. Also, to his chagrin, he found that many of the daily expenses of his department had to be met out of his own pocket. And living in Canada was much more expensive than he had anticipated.

Peter and Elizabeth were no sooner settled in a house in Newark, when Simcoe moved the capital to York and asked Peter to go with him. In 1795 Peter bought Christopher Robinson's small house near the Parliament Buildings and engaged Samuel Marther, a contractor, to enlarge the little house by adding wings and an upper floor. In January 1797 the house burned down due to the carelessness of the workmen who had left a fire burning in an adjoining building where lumber was stored. This meant a loss of £400 and a delay of many months.

Meanwhile, Simcoe had left the country in 1796, and Peter, as senior government official and member of both Executive and Legislative Councils, was appointed President of the Council and Administrator. For the next three years he headed the provisional government, enjoying a plurality of offices which would have been an inspiration to Gilbert and Sullivan. It was President Russell who on June 1, 1797, convened the first Parliament held at York.

Peter owned a water lot at the southwest corner of Palace and Princes Streets in front of the lot where his first house had burned down. The east end of Front Street was called Palace Street because the Government Palace was expected to be built there. The present Princess Street was then called Princes Street. He engaged William Berczy, founder of a German colony at Markham, to build a new house near the Bay shore. They soon quarrelled over delays and high costs. (He paid Berczy £953 for building the house, which included materials.) The garrison blacksmith fashioned all the nails and iron hinges, locks for doors and windows, and bars for the many fireplaces. Peter called the house "Russell Abbey" in memory of Woburn Abbey, seat of the head of the Russell family.

Russell Abbey faced south to the Bay. It was frame, roofed with shingles twenty-seven inches long. The townspeople considered it elegant, although some thought it too pretentious. It was the finest in that part of town, commodious and dignified, though only one storey high — as were most eighteenth century houses in York. It was fifty feet wide, well proportioned, and well adapted for the extensive entertaining expected of the Administrator.

In November 1797 Peter and Elizabeth moved in. The following September Peter wrote to Chief Justice Osgoode, who had moved from York to Quebec, "I have a very comfortable house near the Bay, whence I see everything in the harbour and entering it, and Miss Russell has an extensive poultry yard, which keeps her amused — the expense of living most enormous."

"I hear that you are not snug but actually magnificent in your palace," Osgoode replied.

The house was built in the shape of an H, consisting of a central section with a closed-in porch in the middle, and a gabled wing on each side. There was a large window in the front of each wing, giving the house six windows in the façade, and three windows in the outer walls of the wings. A wide clapboard, always painted white, covered the walls, and a pediment above the windows, similar to that above the porch, lent a touch of elegance. There was no separate dining room; one of the parlours was used at meal times. Miss Russell's diary frequently refers to "the small parlour" and to the footman.

Various outbuildings completed the establishment. The coach-house next to the stable held a light, four-wheeled phaeton with two seats. A low stone wall, surmounted by a wooden fence, enclosed the grounds.

Peter owned a large mineral collection, and his brief study of physic had given him a taste for experiment. He had an isolated building in the rear of Russell Abbey fitted up as a chemical laboratory, and it was this interest in science which led to a warm friendship with Dr. William Warren Baldwin in spite of the difference in their ages. Elizabeth's journal mentions their efforts (unsuccessful) to assemble a microscope.

Under Elizabeth's direction there were soon smooth lawns and excellent gardens at Russell Abbey. She was well informed about herbs,

The Honourable Peter Russell and his sister Elizabeth. Russell amassed enormous land holdings in and around Toronto, and, although scrupulously honest, was often accused of being too greedy in his land acquisitions.

— Ontario Archives

and her wide variety was in great demand for remedies, poultices, and potions. Her diary makes frequent references to entertaining friends in the garden where she served tea and where the gentlemen enjoyed a game of lawn-bowls. She was proud of her flowering shrubs and "laylocks."

Most officials had their offices in their homes. Russell Abbey, too, had a large room fitted up as Peter's office, where his secretary, Joseph Willcocks, a distant relative, worked. Joseph also lived in the house, and in 1800 wrote his brother in Dublin: "I dread the winter, although I have one of the most comfortable rooms in this province . . . we have an elegant pair of horses and a sled that will be fine sport in winter. . . ."

Officials from out of town frequently stayed with Peter Russell, president of the Council, and friends Robert Baldwin and his son Dr.

Baldwin, were always welcome when they came to York from their home in Clarke Township.

In spite of his able administration and devotion to duty, Russell encountered much criticism from younger officials, impatient with his cautious, methodical ways. He was a practical man when the young colony's various problems needed a practical man. He reorganized the complicated land-granting system, and wisely averted trouble with the Indians, and he handled the finances of the province conscientiously. When it became known in 1799 that Simcoe would not return, he expected to be appointed Lieutenant Governor. Simcoe attempted to intercede on his behalf, but by then had little influence. Russell was bitterly disappointed when General Peter Hunter came out as Governor. Hunter ignored Russell as much as he could, even though Russell remained Receiver General — and it was Hunter who initiated much of the spiteful talk about Russell's large land grants, although part of Russell's salary was paid in land, which he was unable to sell.

As Peter's influence declined, he began to spend more and more time in his solitary experiments, until his mysterious activities led some to suspect he was practising witchcraft!

Peter was interested in farming, and on his park lot he used the most improved methods. The farm, called "Petersfield," ran north from modern Queen Street to Bloor Street east of Spadina Avenue. In 1798 he built a comfortable house there, a little north of the corner of modern Soho Street and by the next year had cleared about thirty acres. He cut a road from Russell's Creek, and his approach northward to his farm became known as Peter Street. It was for some time the western boundary of the town.

In 1808 Elizabeth received two proposals. In March her seventy-two-year-old cousin, William Willcocks, father of Dr. Baldwin's wife Phoebe, wrote her a note, "We having both agreed on our closer union, the sooner it can be accomplished the better. I am old and you are not growing younger. . . ."

"The answer to your extraordinary letter is that I think you have taken leave of your senses and beg you will not trouble me any more with such folly and nonsense," Elizabeth replied. In her diary she wrote, "Poor Mrs. Willcocks has not been dead a year and the family are still in mourning for her." Later she added, "The Old Fool came as usual to dinner. . . . I was as cool and distant as possible and avoided being alone with him or even look at him."

In September 1808 Peter died. He left all his possessions to Elizabeth, and she made little attempt to sell anything. In November Robert Baldwin, aged sixty-seven, wrote her a proposal, saying that he had long esteemed her, but fearing that since she was now an heiress she might misinterpret his motives. "Let whatever lawyer you please put your entire fortune beyond my reach. . . . Keep it in your own power. . . ," he declared. We do not know how Elizabeth replied, but the close relationship between her and the Baldwin family did not change. She continued to be friendly with Robert, but remained a spinster.

During the War of 1812, Dr. William Warren Baldwin and his family moved into Russell Abbey with Elizabeth. Dr. Baldwin, who was also a lawyer, had his law office in the Receiver General's former office, and he helped Elizabeth manage her affairs.

When she died in 1822 Elizabeth left everything but a few small legacies to her cousins Phoebe and Maria Willcocks.

In 1831 Russell Abbey was rented to Alexander Macdonnell, the Roman Catholic Bishop, who lived there for about a year. John Munns then occupied the east wing while the west wing remained vacant.

In September 1836 Dr. Baldwin wrote to his son Robert in England, "Mrs. Humphries, mother of Colonel Foster, has taken half of Russell Abbey for £50 a year to open a little boys' school." Very soon afterwards, however, Dr. Bradley rented the entire house and carried on an immigration agency there for about ten years. The last occupants were a Negro family called Truss, who rented the house and established a shoemaking business in it.

In October 1856, when the Honourable Robert Baldwin was the owner, Russell Abbey burned down. All that remains today to remind us of the Russell home is a short street, between Sherbourne and Princess Street north of Front Street, called Abbey Lane.

Davenport
1797-1913

Cities with hills usually develop an exclusive residential area on the hilltops — perhaps because of the view, perhaps because the air is purer, perhaps because we have an unconscious desire to be above our neighbours. Or, perhaps it is a holdover from former times when man felt safer in a hilltop fortress.

The hill area of York was a long way outside of town, but gradually a string of fine homes grew up along the ridge above the old Indian trail which wound in a northwesterly direction from the Don to the Humber rivers. Davenport was the first house on the hill, then Spadina, then Russell Hill, followed by Chestnut Park, Rathnelly, Oaklands, Glen Edyth, Wychwood, and Benvenuto. These were the largest and grandest. Each builder tried to outshine the other, but a man named Pellatt ended the rivalry once and for all when he built a ninety-eight-room castle of baronial splendor, complete with turrets, spectacular lookouts, and secret passages.

The land between Bathurst and Yonge Streets from the 2nd Concession (Bloor) to the 3rd Concession (St. Clair) was divided into five farm lots of two hundred acres each. The westernmost strip, lot 25 in the 2nd Concession from the Bay, was granted to Ensign John McGill on September 4, 1793. McGill had joined the British Army in 1768 and in 1793 was Adjutant of the reorganized Queen's Rangers in Upper Canada. (Ensign McGill is not to be confused with Captain John McGill, the Commissary General, whose house on his park lot is now the site of the Metropolitan United Church.)

Davenport was the first house built on the hill north of York. It commanded an unbroken view over the forest to Lake Ontario.

— Metropolitan Toronto Library Board

In order to qualify for the patent to his lot, McGill cleared a piece of land and built a small house on it. He received his patent in 1798, and we assume that the original Davenport was built in 1797.

We next hear of Davenport in the summer of 1819, when Dr. Baldwin of nearby Spadina writes his friend Quetton St. George that a Major Loring is living at Davenport. Presumably McGill had died and Mrs. McGill had rented the farm and was living in her York town house.

In 1821 Widow McGill sold the two-hundred-acre farm to Colonel Joseph Wells for £750.

Lieutenant Colonel Wells, born in 1773, was a veteran of the Peninsular War, where he had served under the Duke of Wellington and had won the Gold Cross. After Waterloo he came to Canada for a stint as an inspecting field officer, but soon retired to England on half pay. He returned to Canada in 1820.

Colonel Wells liked the small house and the farm perched high on the hill above the Indian trail which cut across the middle of the lot. Besides being a beautiful spot, the site was free of the exasperating swarms of mosquitoes so virulent in the swampy area at the mouth of the Don River, where York was struggling to develop.

If modern Howland Avenue were continued north, its intersection with Austin Terrace would be the approximate site of Davenport. The approach to the house was west from Yonge Street along the Indian trail and up a private drive just east of the present Bathurst Street. The lot line between Spadina and Davenport lies on the west side of the present Walmer Road Hill, at the foot of the sharp bank.

Davenport enjoyed a magnificent view over the forest to Lake Ontario. On a clear day the Wells family could see far out over the lake.

Here Colonel Wells built a new house, much larger than the McGill farmhouse. The new Davenport was a roughcast building of two-and-a-half storeys in the Georgian style. The impression was one of simple dignity and comfort. It stood back a little way from the crest of the hill, and a flight of 120 wooden steps led down the steep hill to the road.

Joseph de Pencier, a great grandson of Colonel Wells, has supplied many descriptive details about Davenport. He remembers that he and his brothers used to ride their bicycles around the house on the roof of the verandah! It was evidently flatter than it appears in the photograph.

After his years in the Army, Colonel Wells enjoyed country living and improving his new property. He rented part of it to a tenant farmer for £1 a year per acre. He planted ten acres of orchards in the back, with

---

Colonel Joseph Wells, a veteran of Waterloo, loved country life. He built a new Davenport and greatly improved the property.

— Metropolitan Toronto Library Board

farm fields farther north. The stables and outbuildings were in the back of the house on the west side.

Colonel Wells was handsome and tall, with a military bearing and a charming manner. He wore his hair in the old-fashioned queue or braid until he died. According to Henry Scadding, that invaluable source of early Toronto history, Mrs. Wells, formerly Harriet King, whom Wells married in 1813, was a "special model of grace and elegance in person and manners." They had eight sons and two daughters, but the girls and three of the boys died as children.

Although York was about six miles away and roads were a test of stamina for both horses and humans, the Colonel took a fairly active part in the political life of the province. He was appointed to the Legislative Council, and in 1825 he acted on a commission investigating claims for losses in the War of 1812. When King's College, forerunner of the University of Toronto, was founded in 1827, he became its first Bursar, a post he held for twelve years. In 1829 he was appointed to the Executive Council, and in the same year he became the first Bursar of the newly established Upper Canada College.

In 1853 Colonel Wells died. The following year his eldest son, who was unmarried, also died. The estate was divided into three long strips from north to south: the strip next to Bathurst Street went to Arthur, the fifth son, and the middle strip went to Robert, the second son, who died in 1868. Robert's widow, Elizabeth Young, and her children remained at Davenport until 1894, even after she married William Wakefield. (Colonel Wells's third son, Charles, drowned when he was only nine years old.)

The eastern strip of the property, 440 feet wide, on which the house and buildings stood, was inherited by Frederick, the fourth son. He had had a distinguished army career during the Crimean War and was decorated by both the French Emperor and the Sultan of Turkey. Toronto, proud of this native son, presented him with a richly decorated Sword of Honour, which joined other Wells trophies on the walls of Davenport.

In 1866 Frederick Wells married Georgina, daughter of George Dartnell, the Surgeon Major of his old regiment. Five years later Frederick retired and settled at Davenport to enjoy his inheritance. Gradually, however, for reasons which are not clear, all the land south of Davenport Road was sold.

A son, George, was born in 1873. Two years later Frederick's wife died giving birth to a daughter, Nina Frederica. After this tragedy Frederick did not wish to remain at Davenport and moved to England with his two infant children. In 1877 he died.

George squandered his money, and Nina inherited Davenport as her share of her father's estate. An orphan since the age of two, she had been reared by a maiden aunt until she was nineteen years old. She then returned to Toronto. (During these years Davenport had been occupied by Mr. and Mrs. Wakefield and her sons Robert and Charles Wells.)

After her return to Toronto, Nina taught Sunday school at St. Alban's Cathedral. Here she met a young curate, Adam Urias de Pencier. They fell in love, were married in 1895, and lived in Davenport for nearly ten years. They then moved to Manitoba and later to British Columbia, where Adam de Pencier became Archbishop, and subsequently Metropolitan of British Columbia.

From 1909 until 1912 Davenport was rented to a John O. Thorn. By this time the property had shrunk to twenty acres, and in 1913 Nina de Pencier sold it. The land was subdivided and Davenport was demolished.

Today only names remind us of the fine old family who lived there: Davenport Road, Wells Avenue, Dupont Street, Nina Street, Wells Hill Avenue, Wells Hill Park and Dartnell Avenue.

Beverley House

1812-1912

The house was demolished long ago, but one can still walk through its front door, through which Toronto's pillars of government and society once came and went. The door, with its brass knocker, fanlight, and sidelights, is on display at the Royal Ontario Museum.

Just before the outbreak of the War of 1812 D'Arcy Boulton Jr. built a one-storey brick house near the southwest corner of the square bounded by the present Queen, John, Richmond, and Simcoe Streets. Set in virgin forest, the little house was far to the west of the settled part of York. About 1817 John Beverley Robinson, whose sister Sarah was married to D'Arcy, bought the property and named it "Beverley House."

John was the son of Christopher Robinson, of a distinguished military and legal Virginian family, originally from Yorkshire. At the outbreak of the American Revolution Christopher went to stay with his uncle, Colonel Beverley Robinson. The house was on the Hudson River opposite West Point, and its name was "Beverley House." There, Christopher was commissioned in Colonel J.G. Simcoe's Legion (later the Queen's Rangers). Because of Colonel Robinson's loyalty to the Crown, his home and 60,000 acres were later confiscated.

Christopher, too, lost his Virginia wealth and after the war moved to Lower Canada. His son John was born there in 1791. In 1798 Christopher moved to York, where he died at the age of thirty-four. His son

Beverley House, the home of Emma and John Robinson, the Attorney General. York society was both amused and scandalized by Anne Powell's relentless pursuit of the dignified Robinson.

— Metropolitan Toronto Library Board

John was sent to Dr. Strachan's new school in Cornwall. John was a brilliant student and he and Strachan became friends. Their friendship was to last for sixty years.

John was a law student in the office of Attorney General John Macdonnell when the War of 1812 erupted. Macdonnell became aide-de-camp to General Brock and John a lieutenant in the York Militia. He fought at Queenston Heights where both Macdonnell and their gallant leader Brock were killed. Soon after John became Acting Attorney General, although he had not yet been called to the Bar. After the war he was appointed Solicitor General.

Chief Justice W.D. Powell used his influence to get John's appointments, and York gossips noticed that his daughter Anne was acting as if betrothed to John, although he gave her no encouragement. Pretty, witty, headstrong Anne, four years older than John, was infatuated with John's good looks and charming manners and refused to listen to her embarrassed parents' pleas for restraint.

In 1816 John went to England and was admitted to the English Bar. In 1817 he met and married Emma Walker. They returned to York, bought Boulton's little cottage, and started to improve it. They added a second storey and a large wing on the west side. A verandah supported by slender columns was built across the front, with a small balcony above the front door. The house was covered with white roughcast (coarser than modern stucco). Stables and a coach house were built on the northwest corner of the grounds, with a rear entrance from Queen Street.

Since John's brother-in-law, D'Arcy Boulton Jr., was at this time also building The Grange and his friend Reverend John Strachan his mansion, one may assume that animated discussions took place concerning the various plans for their houses. In fact, the houses were similar in many ways.

Beverley House faced south to the lake and had a centre hall plan. A gravel drive swept in a long curve to the front door and a sundial on a square stone stood on the lawn. A high brick wall enclosed the property, except on Richmond Street (then Hospital Street) where the front gates were set in a wrought-iron fence above a low wall. A tiny stream ran along the west side of the house, while on the east side gardens — vegetables, berry bushes, and roses — flourished.

The library contained ceiling-high walnut bookshelves and a high carved desk. Three-cornered chairs and a big sofa were covered with bright red damask, matching the window drapes. One armchair was covered with glossy, very slippery horsehair.

The dining room's rear door had a long curtain to screen the comings and goings of servants from the basement kitchen. Many memorable dinners were held in this room. Top government officials, society ladies, and famous visitors dined here. Charles Dickens, while on his lecture tour, was a guest.

The double drawing room was divided by a square arch which could be closed by heavy drapes; fireplaces with handsome walnut mantels stood in every room. The wide hallway was hung with antlered trophies, armour, and weapons. The stairs curved near the top, where a

Anne Powell, the headstrong daughter of Chief Justice W.D. Powell, and John Beverley Robinson, the man she pursued.

— W.R. Riddell, *Life of William Dummer Powell*, 1924
— Metropolitan Toronto Library Board

walnut box, fastened to the railing, held a lamp. The shallow steps were painted cream, in contrast to the black walnut of the banister and newel posts. It was a house built to last.

John's marriage had made little difference to Anne Powell who pursued him as before, although Emma refused to admit her to Beverley House. Anne wrote what John's brother called "the damndest letters," and her behaviour was trying to the dignified Robinson, who in 1818 had become Attorney General. York society was both amused and scandalized.

Early in 1822 John was appointed a commissioner and sent to England on a mission. Anne declared that she would accompany him and Emma. Anne's father, Chief Justice Powell, was in England, and her mother could not dissuade her. Mrs. Powell called on Dr. Strachan to reason with her, and Anne's brother locked up her luggage, and, according to an unconfirmed story, tied her to a bedpost. Undaunted, Anne bribed a servant, escaped, and rushed to Kingston by sleigh, then on to Albany, New York, where she caught up with the Robinsons. She travelled with them to New York, writing triumphantly to her mother that she was considered "the lady of the party." Robinson, however, refused to let Anne accompany them on the ship. She was forced to stay in New York with an uncle.

But she did set out for England later, ostensibly to join her father. Her ship *Albion* ran into a storm off Ireland and poor Anne Powell drowned.

In 1830, at the age of thirty-nine, John was appointed Chief Justice and President of the Executive Council.

When the new Governor General, Lord Sydenham, came to Toronto in 1839 to implement Lord Durham's suggested union of the Canadas, he found the Lieutenant Governor living at Government House, and had to look for other quarters. Robinson was on leave in England (publishing a criticism of the Union), and Sydenham took over Beverley House. It became the vice-regal residence with sentries at the entrance and aides rushing in and out. In order to properly entertain councillors and Assembly members, Sydenham built a huge new kitchen with an enormous stove.

So it was that the Act of Union was debated in the dining room of Robinsons' house, where excellent dinners and fine wines did their work — in spite of the opposition of Strachan and his friends — and it was in the drawing room before the fireplace that the draft of the new constitution was hammered out. The bill was passed, and, when Britain passed the Canada Act, Upper and Lower Canada found themselves united.

The Robinsons had four sons and four daughters, and after they came back from England, Beverley House was filled with gaiety and activity. The daughters' weddings were great social events, especially that of Augusta Ann to Bishop Strachan's son, James. A charming portrait by Berthon of the three eldest daughters was commissioned by the three sons-in-law and presented to the Robinsons as a surprise. It hung in Beverley House for many years. Today it is in The Grange.

A dozen small red leather notebooks, now in the Ontario Archives, record the Robinsons' household expenses. Details of everyday life appear. From the 1854 notebook one notes that four gallons of sherry cost £6/3, one dozen champagne £4/6, spectacles for Mr. R., 10 shillings, three waistcoats for Charles £1/6. The cost of servants? Footman £2/15 per month, plus coats, gloves, and aprons; coachman £3 per month, Hannah £2 plus shoes, cook £2, housemaid 25 shillings, gardener 5 shillings a day. Extra help — waiters, needlewomen, and charwomen — are also mentioned.

In 1853 Chief Justice Robinson became the first Chancellor of the University of Trinity College; and the next year he was made a baronet. In 1863 he died. Two years later, Lady Robinson died. Their third son, Christopher, a prominent lawyer, inherited Beverley House. He had been born there in 1828, and he lived there until his death in 1905.

Christopher modernized the house. The long front verandah was removed and a square porch with a small balcony was added. The ornate balustrade of the early balcony was replaced by a simple wooden railing. A larger porch and balcony were added on the east side, and a sunroom was built on the west side.

During Christopher's time the first street west of John Street was named Beverley Street, and a small hotel called "Beverley House" opened on the northwest corner of Beverley and Queen Streets. One can imagine the amusement and perhaps the annoyance which this shabby hostelry, one short block from their mansion, must have caused the family.

After Christopher died, his widow and family stayed on until 1912. In 1912 the old house, scene of a thousand brilliant gatherings, was demolished, and the Methodist Book Room was built in its place. But part of the old brick wall managed to survive until 1954, when Ryerson Press built its headquarters on Queen Street and tore it down also.

Mrs. Christopher Robinson built a larger replica of Beverley House on the south side of St. Clair Avenue, west of Walmer Road. It, too, was stucco over brick. The solid front door, with its bronze knocker, fanlight, sidelights, and inner shutters, was installed in the new house. The walnut panelling, bookshelves, and mantelpiece from the

The double drawing room of Beverley House. Note the square arch which divided the two halves, and the handsome walnut mantels.

— Metropolitan Toronto Library Board

original library were moved to the new library. The fireplaces from the drawing room were also saved, as were three gilded chandeliers.

In 1921 Horace B. Smith, a lawyer with shipbuilding interests, bought the house and renamed it "Hawkherst." In 1940 he died. His daughter, Mrs. Gerald Greene, and her family lived in the house for two more years. She then sold it to the Ursuline Order of nuns who opened a school there. In 1966 the Ursulines bought Colonel Clifford

The cluttered hallway of Beverley House was hung in the Victorian style with antlered trophies, armour, and weapons.
— Metropolitan Toronto Library Board

Sifton's house on Lawrence Avenue at Bayview and moved the school there. Hawkherst was demolished.

The walnut panelling and bookshelves of Beverley House were moved once more to the Sifton house library. And, again, the beautiful front door was rescued and placed in the Canadiana Gallery of the Royal Ontario Museum, where it is today — a solid reminder of one of Toronto's great houses.

Belle Vue
1815-1890

The Denison family built a number of memorable houses in early Toronto — Brookdale, Belle Vue, Dover Court, Rush Holme, and Heyden Villa. One of the earliest was Belle Vue.

George Taylor Denison, eldest son of Captain John Denison and Sophia Taylor, inherited from his father a great deal of land in York and Weston. Thanks to his good management and the substantial dowries of his four wives, he eventually owned a vast amount of property in Toronto and its suburbs.

George was born in England in 1783. In 1792 he came to Canada with his parents. In 1806 he married Esther Borden, the fifteen-year-old only child of Captain Richard Lippincott, a United Empire Loyalist who had settled on a three-thousand-acre grant near Richmond Hill.

In 1815 George inherited Park Lot 17 and the east half of Park Lot 18 — a total of 156 acres extending from modern Queen Street to Bloor Street between Lippincott and Major Streets, as now laid out. He immediately began to build his house on a site a short distance east of the present Western Hospital.

Belle Vue was a large, comfortable house of white roughcast, facing south. It was about half a mile north of Queen Street but was clearly visible up the long carriage drive cut through the dense forest. This avenue, beneath trees which met overhead, was called "Denison's Avenue" (today Denison Avenue).

Belle Vue's four sides faced squarely to the four points of the compass — the front faced due south, the back due north.

— Metropolitan Toronto Library Board

Belle Vue was typical of the Loyalist Georgian style of architecture popular in Upper Canada at this time. A rectangle with a narrow cornice, its wide front displayed a balanced symmetry — five windows of twenty small panes each in the second storey, and two longer windows of twenty-four panes each on each side of the front door in the lower storey. All windows had dark green shutters, a pleasant contrast to the white roughcast of the walls.

An open porch of slender pillars and graceful pediment protected the front door, which, like the hallway, was hospitably wide. As in many English town houses of the day, the drawing room was on the second floor.

George Taylor Denison, builder of Belle Vue, had, like many other members of his family, a distinguished military career, and because of inheritances and the substantial dowries of his four wives, he eventually owned a vast amount of property in and around Toronto.

— Metropolitan Toronto Library Board

Belle Vue's four sides faced squarely to the points of the compass, said to be the only house in Toronto so built. The front of the house faced due south and the back due north. (Its exact location today would be the northeast corner of Denison Avenue and Denison Square.)

George Taylor Denison, the first of that name, had a distinguished military career. He served in the War of 1812 as a militia officer in the York Volunteers, and in 1822 he organized a volunteer cavalry troop which he maintained at considerable personal expense until 1837. He commanded this troop, known as Denison's Horse, during the Rebellion of 1837. Later the troop was expanded and became the Governor General's Body Guard. Many of its early officers were Denisons, and many of the fine horses were owned by Denisons. It is interesting to note that the first eight commanding officers, and one later, were Denisons. This regiment, now known as the Governor General's Horse Guards, has lost its horses (except for a ceremonial escort troop) — but it still has a Denison among its officers.

In 1838 George Taylor Denison, an extremely handsome and imposing man, was gazetted Lieutenant Colonel of the 3rd York Battalion. In 1846 he assumed command of the 4th Battalion of Toronto militia, which he retained until his death in 1853.

By his first wife, Esther, he had eight children — five born at Weston, three at Belle Vue. Two boys and a daughter died in infancy, but Sophia, Eliza, George, Mary, and Robert survived.

Esther died in 1823, at thirty-one. When Denison was in England four years later, he married his first cousin, Maria Taylor of Dover Court, by whom he had one son, who died in infancy.

Maria Taylor died in 1831. In 1833 Denison married a widow, Mrs. Todd, who had been Elizabeth Caldwell. Of this marriage four children were born at Belle Vue — Eliza died in infancy; Georgina was born in 1837, John in 1839, and Charles Leslie in 1841. When John was fourteen years old, he was fatally shot by his younger brother Charles while Charles was playing with a new rifle.

Elizabeth, the third wife, died in 1849. The following year Denison married Maria Priscilla Coates. This marriage was childless.

In 1853 Colonel George Taylor Denison died. When his will was probated his estate was found to be the largest in Ontario to that date.

Elizabeth Caldwell had inherited a great deal of land, most of which went to young Charles.

The older sons, Richard Lippincott and George Taylor 2nd, already had their share at Dover Court and Rush Holme, and so Robert Brittain, born in 1821, inherited Belle Vue. In 1845 he had married Emily Winn of London, England, and was living in a modest house on the east side of Denison Avenue near Queen Street. Robert found that much of the Belle Vue property had already been disposed of. The half north of College Street had been sold, and small blocks in the southern half were inherited by his sisters.

Robert, like his father and brothers, was keenly interested in horses and military life. Although an accident had robbed him of one eye, he became a Lieutenant Colonel, the fourth Commanding Officer of the Governor General's Body Guard.

In 1857 Colonel Denison, who was a church warden and supporter of St. George's Church on John Street, built St. Stephen's (Anglican) Church on his Belle Vue property. This charming stone church, originally called St. Stephen's-in-the-Fields at what is now the southeast corner of College Street and Bellevue Avenue, is similar to the Church of the Redeemer at Bloor and Avenue Road. St. Stephen's was built and maintained entirely at his expense and, when it was completely destroyed by fire in 1865, Robert rebuilt it exactly as it had been.

It is said that Robert differed from the first rector of St. Stephen's Church, H.J. McCallum, on some theological points. When the rector refused to yield to his church's builder, Robert and his family attending service would wait until the rector rose to preach, then would all rise and march out. This weekly disturbance led the rector to say, "This vexes me so much that I am unable to preach." A note signed by Robert Denison soon appeared on the church door, "You never could."

Colonel Denison lived until 1900, having in 1889 sold what remained of the Belle Vue property. The handsome old house was demolished in 1890. Today Bellevue Park occupies the site.

Streets named Denison, Bellevue, Borden, Lippincott, Augusta, and Esther commemorate the Denisons of Belle Vue.

The Bishop's Palace
1817-1900

Not built expressly as the official residence of the Anglican Bishop of Toronto, The Bishop's Palace was the home of the Reverend John Strachan. He built it, owned it, and lived in it for fifty years. No other clergyman ever occupied it.

John Strachan, son of a Scottish stonemason, arrived in Upper Canada on the last day of the eighteenth century. He was twenty-one years old, short but handsome, well educated, quick tempered, and domineering. He had a harsh Aberdonian accent. He was also a Presbyterian and he was penniless. He had been chosen to head a college at Kingston but when this failed to materialize, he stayed in Kingston to tutor the sons of the Honourable Richard Cartwright, and lived with the Cartwright family.

In 1803 he opened a grammar school in Cornwall, where he taught the sons of the Establishment. By this time he had seen the light and had been converted to the Church of England. In 1804 he became a clergyman.

In 1804, too, Strachan was courting Anne, the pretty daughter of Dr. George Wood. She had also attracted Andrew McGill, brother and partner of Montreal merchant James McGill. The wealthy McGill, thirty-two years older than Anne, proposed and promised to leave her well provided. Strachan is alleged to have advised her to accept, saying he would wait. Anne and Andrew McGill married and moved to Montreal. Andrew died in 1805, and Anne, a widow and heiress at nineteen, returned to her father's home in Cornwall.

When The Bishop's Palace was built in 1817 it was the most impressive house in town. The front door had no exterior door knob since a gentleman's door would, of course, be opened by a servant.

— Metropolitan Toronto Library Board

Strachan and Anne were married by the Reverend John Bethune in Williamstown in May 1807. The marriage was a happy one. (Some years later James McGill, at Strachan's suggestion, provided funds to found McGill University.)

"I had almost forgot to tell you, that seeing no prospect of my ever being able to return home, I married last spring and find myself happy in this connexion. My wife has an annuity of 300 [pounds] a year for life. She has a great share of beauty . . . and as good an education as this country can afford, which by the way, is not great. . . ," Strachan wrote his friend Dr. James Brown at the University of Glasgow. Anne's name was not mentioned.

When, at the suggestion of Sir Isaac Brock, Strachan moved to York in June 1812, it was as Rector of York and Chaplain to the troops and the Legislative Council. Soon he was headmaster of the York Grammar School (the Blue School) and a member of the powerful Executive Council. His advancement was rapid. His influence spread beyond the Church into the fields of education and politics and he became a pillar of the Family Compact.

When Americans captured York in 1813, it was Strachan who faced General Dearborn, the American Commander, and demanded that he halt the sack of the town. The invaders had already burned the Parliament Buildings and pillaged the church, and York had John Strachan to thank that it was not burned to the ground.

In 1815 the rented house which he occupied was destroyed by fire — his second house to go by fire. Strachan then determined to build his own home, which would be large enough for his growing family and fine enough for entertaining on a lavish scale. In August 1816 he bought a town lot from Alexander McDonnell, executor of former Solicitor General R.I.D. Gray, which occupied the block of land on Front Street, from York Street west to Graves Street (now called Simcoe) and north to Market Street (now Wellington).

In 1817 Strachan began to build a large house on the north side of Front Street. It was sixty-six feet wide and forty feet deep, and made of red bricks manufactured on the spot. This was the third brick building in York, and the first house to use locally burned bricks. Even the inner partitions of the lower storey were brick. The lodgehouse at the entrance to the grounds and a high wall surrounding the property were of the same brick.

When Chief Justice W.D. Powell, who occupied a smaller house across York Street, saw Strachan's house going up, he remarked sourly that it was a "palace being built in anticipation of a mitre."

With a sharp eye Strachan supervised every stage of the building, demanding superior materials and workmanship. The result was a mansion in late neoclassical style, the most impressive house in town — truly a palace compared to the other houses. Immediately, the sparsely settled neighbourhood became fashionable.

The house was similar to two other brick houses built about the same time — The Grange and Mr. Justice Campbell's house on Duke Street. Strachan's house, however, was much wider than the Campbell house, having seven windows in the second storey, where the Duke Street house had five. A contemporary account describes it as "of capacious dimensions and good design, with extensive and complete appurtenances."

Set well back from the street, it faced south, commanding an unobstructed view of the Bay. A low central gable, with a semi-circular window, broke the long line of the roof. A square-pillared porch led to a double front door, hospitably wide. The doors, of solid walnut, had a high, elliptical fanlight and there was no exterior door knob, since a gentleman's door would, of course, be opened by a servant. A handsome Palladian window in the upper hall above the front door contributed to the air of dignity and superb taste. Its proud owner declared it the "best-appointed private establishment in the province."

In a letter to his brother James in December 1818, Strachan said the house had cost £2,500, but that he valued it at £5,000. His words could have been written in any century: "My house has cost me more money than I expected, and when to this I add the furnishing of it, I find myself nearly £2,000 in debt. This I shall clear away, if God spare me a few years, and then I shall be the best lodged man in Canada." He had borrowed heavily from his brother to buy imported furniture and pictures.

When Lieutenant Governor Gore left Canada in 1818, Strachan bought much of Gore's fine furniture at the auction sale. According to Mrs. W.D. Powell, wife of the Chief Justice, "It gives Dr. Strachan an opportunity of furnishing his most elegant mansion, which is the handsomest and largest in the province. Ours, more suitable to our wants and my wishes, is not suitable for such expensive luxuries."

Strachan wrote to Gore, "We are in our new house, and find it delightful. It was my intention to wait a year or two to furnish it, but wives are impatient. The expense has involved me considerably. . . ."

The house had a gracious centre hall, with a wide, shallow staircase. Because of fine proportions and high ceilings there was a sense of spaciousness. Much of the interior woodwork was black walnut. A formal drawing room to the right of the front door was "cold and stiff, with many ornaments under glass shades, a marble-topped table and thick

John Strachan (1779-1867). His indomitable spirit and firm belief in the rightness of his opinions exercised a strong influence on Upper Canada for two generations.
— Ontario Archives

carpets and curtains," in the words of a grandniece. A small sitting room behind the drawing room was more intimate and comfortable.

Across the hall was the large dining parlour, with its huge dining table and massive furniture. Behind this room was the imposing library, where the master was never to be disturbed. Chairs were covered with rich red velvet.

The Bishop's Palace 61

The same magnificent crimson lent a richness to other rooms. The huge four-poster bed in Mrs. Strachan's room was canopied in crimson, and the large couch at the foot of the bed, where she rested in the afternoon, was covered in the same material.

One room had cream walls with a wide frieze painted in perfect imitation of crimson velvet drapery, looped with tassels and cords. This room was considered one of the most elegant in York.

Henry Scadding in his *Toronto of Old* relates that when Strachan's brother James visited him from Aberdeen, he was much impressed by the fine new house, and with sly humour remarked, "I hope it's a' come by honestly, John!" This story has been much embroidered in later accounts.

The large house always seemed filled with children (four were born there, although the two Emmas died in infancy), visiting relatives, and dignitaries.

In 1833 Strachan sold a strip from the eastern side of his land to Thomas Mercer Jones, Commissioner of the Canada Company, who had recently married Elizabeth Mary, the only one of Strachan's four daughters to live to maturity. He built a charming Regency villa facing York Street and called it "The Cottage."

At this time the York Directory described the south side of Market Street, west of York Street, as "Gardens and backfront of the mansion of the Hon. and Venerable John Strachan, D.D. Archdeacon of York."

During his half-century occupation of the house, Strachan wrote many letters and papers in his large, comfortable library, and the room often witnessed meetings of powerful men. In December 1837 the Lieutenant Governor, Sir Francis Bond Head, and his advisers met in Strachan's study to decide how to cope with the rebels; thus Strachan was able to influence the plan which was adopted, and it was in the grounds of his home that the local militia assembled the next day before marching north to Montgomery's Tavern to meet the "Little Rebel." William Lyon Mackenzie often vilified Strachan as the arch-enemy of reform, and doubtless the dislike was reciprocated.

When in 1839 Strachan became the first Bishop of Toronto, his residence began to be called "The Bishop's Palace," and henceforth was always designated "The Palace."

During the bishop's absence in 1850, Mrs. Strachan, always up-to-date, decided to install gas pipes and fixtures for better illumination. Because of the danger of noxious fumes and the possibility of serious accidents through the ignorance of servants, her innovation was criticized by friends and relatives.

Among many splendid entertainments at The Palace, the most outstanding was that given for Albert Edward, Prince of Wales, when he visited Toronto in 1860. Bishop and Mrs. Strachan had become famous for their lavish hospitality, and this was a magnificent occasion.

Bishop Strachan, whose indomitable spirit and firm belief in the rightness of his opinions exercised a strong influence on the whole province for two generations, died in 1867. He was in his ninetieth year, and only one of his eight children, Captain James McGill Strachan, survived him. Mrs. Strachan had died two years before.

The Palace was occupied briefly by the newly founded Bishop Strachan School, then rented as a private hotel, called, naturally, "The Palace Hotel." Gradually the fine old house grew shabby, its grounds neglected and shrunken by sales around its perimeter. The splendid view of Lake Ontario was obstructed by the first Union Station, built in 1858.

The house was bought by Sir John Carling, wealthy brewer from London, Ontario, who rented it to various proprietors. From 1874 on it operated as a boarding house. Eventually, in 1890, the proud old mansion, now known as The Palace Boarding House, was demolished to make way for warehouses. The once fashionable residential street had become an industrial neighbourhood.

John Ross Robertson, editor of *The Evening Telegram*, rescued enough solid oak from the threshold of the front door to make a throne-like chair, which he presented to Trinity University — which Bishop Strachan had founded in 1851.

University Avenue now runs through the site of the Bishop's Palace.

Spadina 1
1818-1835

The handsome house on the brow of the Davenport Hill, east of Casa Loma, is the third house on the site to be called Spadina. The original Spadina was built by Dr. William Warren Baldwin in 1818 on land left to him by his father-in-law, William Willcocks.

Willcocks came to Canada from Ireland in 1792, and, because of his efforts (unsuccessful) to found a colony in Whitby Township, was given large grants of Crown land. Several half-acre town lots in York were granted to his wife and children. Since Willcocks was a first cousin of Peter Russell, the Receiver General, his lands were all in choice locations. He received Park Lot 15, one hundred acres immediately west of Russell's own land, Petersfield. Willcocks also devised to Dr. Baldwin Lot 24 in the 2nd Concession from the Bay, two hundred acres running from modern Bloor Street to St. Clair Avenue, north of his park lot.

William W. Baldwin was the son of Robert Baldwin of County Cork, Ireland. In 1798 Robert brought six of his sixteen children with him to Upper Canada. William, who had graduated in medicine at Edinburgh in 1796, accompanied his father, and in 1802 moved to York.

William was the first civilian doctor in York — there being several army doctors already there. To eke out his tiny income he opened a small private school for boys in the home of William Willcocks, where he boarded. The following year he married Phoebe, his landlord's second daughter. Neither medicine nor schoolmastering were lucrative, so Dr. Baldwin obtained a licence as an attorney. He closed his school and practised both law and medicine.

The Baldwins decided to call their house "Spadina" when they heard the Indians calling the area "Espadinong," meaning a sudden rise of land. The first Spadina house burnt down in 1835. Subsequently two more Spadinas were to occupy the same site.

— Metropolitan Toronto Library Board

For some years Dr. Baldwin lived in York at the corner of Front and Bay Streets. In 1813 Willcocks died and left part of his land to Phoebe. Dr. Baldwin stayed in York, but farmed the land with a tenant farmer who lived in a small house on the property.

On September 22, 1818 Dr. Baldwin wrote to a cousin in Ireland, "Robert is 14 — I am very busy now hurrying on the plastering of the house I have built almost 3 miles from town where I propose to live." The house was on the crest of the hill above an old Indian trail which led to the Humber River. This trail, now Davenport Road, was for some years known as "Dr. Baldwin's Road." When they learned that the Indians called the area by a name which sounded like "espadinong" meaning "a sudden rise of land," the Baldwins decided to call their house and land "Spadina," pronounced "Spadeena," the three syllables accented equally.

North of the house was a deep ravine with a stream flowing southeast. Spadina was rectangular in shape, as were most of the houses of the day, but the front door, instead of being in the middle of the long side, as was usually the case, was placed in the narrow end, on the right side. There was no front porch — the steep steps led up to the door directly from the ground.

There were six windows in the long side in both ground floor and second storey, with two windows in the narrow end on the ground floor, and three windows above. The only architectural embellishment was a semi-oval fanlight above the solid front door.

The basement was high, with numerous windows to light the kitchen, wine cellar, and storerooms. The house was built close against a large wooden building, perhaps an earlier house or barn.

On July 29, 1819 Dr. Baldwin wrote to Quetton St. George, the French Royalist emigré who had built the first brick house in York at the northeast corner of King and Frederick Streets, "I have a very commodious house in the country. . . . I have called the place Spadina, the Indian word for Hill or Mount — the house consists of two large parlours, Hall and staircase on the first floor — four bedrooms and a small library on the second floor — and three excellent bed-rooms in the attic storey or garret — with several closets on every storey — a kitchen, dairy, root-cellar, and man's bed-room underground. I have cut an avenue through the woods all the way so that we can see the vessels passing up and down the Bay — the house is completely finished with stable and a tolerable good garden, the whole has cost about £1500 . . . the land you know was the gift of poor Mr. Willcocks — whom I am sure you will never forget. . . ."

Spadina was not the first house built on the high ridge which had been the shoreline of old Lake Iroquois. Some years previously Adjutant John McGill had built Davenport to the west, and in about 1820 Dr. Baldwin's brother Augustus (later Admiral) finished building Russell Hill on the property east of Spadina.

Dr. Baldwin was on intimate terms with Peter Russell and his sister Elizabeth, acting as their lawyer and physician. Peter left his vast land holdings to Elizabeth, and, when she died in 1822, she left a great deal of land to her young cousins Phoebe Baldwin and Maria Willcocks. Dr. Baldwin was now able to widen and improve the land between Petersfield and the former Willcocks park lot which led from the town to his farm. This splendid avenue, now called Spadina, was for many years the widest street in Toronto. He imported and planted a double row of chestnut trees along the sides.

Some years after moving to Spadina, Dr. Baldwin built a family cemetery called St. Martin's Rood, north of the house.

Maria Willcocks never married. She lived with the Baldwins, and at her death in 1834 her share of Willcocks and Russell property passed to William and Phoebe Baldwin.

In 1835 the first Spadina was completely destroyed by fire. A full documentation of the two subsequent Spadinas can be found in *Spadina, A Story of Old Toronto*, by Austin Seton Thompson.

Rosedale House

1821-1905

Today Rosedale is a subway station, a school, a golf club, a tennis club, a Presbyterian church, a hamburger stand, and many other things. For generations Rosedale was an exclusive residential area of winding streets and Victorian mansions, whose massive dimensions and extensive grounds proclaimed their owners' affluence. Originally, however, Rosedale was a 120-acre farm on the east side of Yonge, north of Bloor Street.

The land was granted by the Crown to a George Playter in 1796, but by 1821 James Small (the son of Major John Small who built Berkeley House and killed Attorney General White in a duel) had bought part of the land and built a house there. Three years later Small sold the property for £200 to William Botsford Jarvis, whose father, Stephen, had served under Colonel Simcoe in the American Revolutionary War. After the war Stephen returned to his native Connecticut. There a mob nearly killed him, but he managed to escape to New Brunswick, where his bride, Amelia Glover, joined him.

Stephen, Amelia, and their six children moved to York in 1809. William was then ten years old. In 1827 William became High Sheriff of the Home District (the present counties of York, Peel, and Ontario), and, after Amelia's death, Stephen lived with him and managed the farm.

In 1828 William married Mary Boyles Powell, granddaughter of Chief Justice William Dummer Powell. When she saw the profusion

Rosedale was the beloved home of the William Jarvis family. Because of the ravines, there were few farm fields and the Jarvis children were free to roam the thickly wooded slopes and to fish in the streams.

— Metropolitan Toronto Library Board

of wild roses which covered the hillsides, Mary gave the name "Rosedale" to her new home. The district has retained the name, although both Rosedale House and the wild roses have long since vanished.

William's position as sheriff took him on long journeys, and Mary took over the management of Rosedale. The house, which had been a bachelor hall, was gradually improved and in time became elegant. Originally Rosedale House was an austere, hip-roofed square block, built of brick, and, like many of the houses of the day, covered by rough stucco. It was two storeys high, with a gently sloping roof and centre-hall plan. The big brick-floored kitchen was in the basement. Romantic in setting, it was built on the crest of a steep hill, southwest of the intersection of today's Cluny Drive and Rosedale Road, facing west to Yonge Street. A long lane (modern Park Road) descended the

Mary Jarvis changed Rosedale from a bachelor hall to a beautiful estate. When she died, her daughter Fanny wrote: "Rosedale's heart grew cold."

— *Mary's Rosedale*, 1928

steep slope from Yonge Street, crossed a primitive bridge over a tumbling stream in the ravine, and wound upward to the house in a northwesterly direction along what is now Rosedale Road.

In the election of 1830, Jarvis defeated Robert Baldwin to represent York in the Assembly, and four years later he was largely responsible for getting the Toronto Incorporation Act through the House, by which the town of York became the city of Toronto.

William and Mary had two sons and three daughters: Anne Frances (Fanny), whose unpublished *Recollections* are so valuable for the story of Rosedale, Mary Louisa, William Dummer, Sarah, and Robert Colborne. On Fanny's fifth birthday Mary planted a small elm tree near the back door. The tree flourished until it became the famous Rosedale Elm, beloved in the neighbourhood by later generations.

About 1835 William opened a new road from Yonge Street, along the present Roxborough Street and down modern Cluny Drive. (The entire road winding south was at one time called Rosedale Road.) He built a lodge at the Yonge Street gate, and planted a fine avenue of trees beside the new road. This approach was a great improvement over the earlier road, which started south of Severn's Brewery, descended into the deep ravine, crossed the creek, and, with the greatest difficulty, climbed the precipitous hill on the other side.

During the Rebellion of 1837 William was away from home commanding a militia regiment. As Mackenzie and his rebel army marched down Yonge Street, Mackenzie remembered that the Jarvis family were members of the hated Family Compact. He decided to burn Rosedale to the ground. Two of the children were sick in bed, and, when Mary saw the flames of a neighbour's house, she sent Wilson, the coachman, for Dr. William Gwynne, her sister Anne's husband. The rebels captured Wilson, but Colonel Lount, one of Mackenzie's officers, said he was not there to fight women and sick children. Together with some of the cooler rebels, he persuaded Mackenzie to spare Rosedale. Lount also sent for Dr. Gwynne. Dr. Gwynne took Mary and her children by a back road around Bloor's millpond and down through the Moss Park property to her grandfather's house at Front and York Streets. Rosedale was spared.

Sheriff William Jarvis and his three daughters, Anne Frances (Fanny), Mary Louisa, and Sarah. The photograph was taken in 1854, soon after Mary died.
— *Mary's Rosedale*, 1928

Meanwhile, William, with twenty-seven men, waited near the present Maitland and Yonge Streets. When they saw the rebels advancing, they opened fire. Mackenzie and his followers, thinking they were regular troops, panicked, and retreated to Gallows Hill.

Mary made Rosedale comfortable and welcoming, and, whenever the Sheriff was home, they entertained frequently, their invitations being much sought after. In 1838 they held a fancy dress ball. Its description in the *Patriot* of the day gives us a glimpse of the house. The large verandah was closed in, with a stove at each end, and the walls were covered with pictures. "This Picture Gallery was lighted by a profusion of coloured lamps, which afforded a spacious and picturesque promenade . . . music and dancing continued to a late hour. . . ."

Mary did not confine her attention to the house, but was also an enthusiastic gardener. Rosedale's rose gardens and orchards were famous, and she laid out gravelled walks with rustic seats and arbours. In addition to the tropical plants in the conservatory, she cultivated peaches and grapes in special small buildings on the sunny side of the house.

Many relatives from England made long visits to Rosedale, and, as the Sheriff's own family grew, he enlarged the house a good deal. An extension with dormer windows in the upper floor was built in the rear, and it is probable that a new kitchen was in this addition.

Jarvis's salary was often slow in arriving. To make ends meet he began to sell pieces of the property. The buyers identified themselves with Rosedale and liked the tone which the name gave their homes. Thus the whole area retained the Rosedale name.

The Rosedale Ravine was an ideal playground for the Jarvis children who caught trout in the roaring creek and damned it up in several places, making wonderful swimming holes. The area was still thickly wooded with magnificent maples, pines, and elms. The millpond of nearby Bloor's Brewery was big enough to float rafts on, and in winter made a good skating rink, while the numerous hills were made for sleighs. Because of the ravines, farm fields were small and scattered.

In 1846 William and Mary rented Rosedale and took the children to England to be educated. Fanny and William spent two years at school in Paris, where they saw some of the excitement of the Revolution of 1848. William returned to Rosedale, and wrote to Mary that he could not get a tenant for the house as it needed repairs and redecorating.

In 1849 there was a serious fire. The barn and outbuildings, including the peach house, burned down, but somehow the house was saved.

In 1851 a large wedding reception was held at Rosedale for Fanny, who married Edmund Meredith, the Irish barrister and principal of McGill University. When he became Provincial Secretary they moved to Quebec. Years later they returned to Rosedale.

In a letter to Fanny in May 1852, Mary writes that Rosedale is in such bad repair that it cannot be occupied. She mentions daily visits to supervise the repairs, and says they are planting evergreens on the Block House hill — red cedars, spruce, hemlock, and fir — to make a forest screen between the house and Yonge Street.

However, William and Mary had barely moved back in when Mary became ill and died. Fanny writes that "Rosedale's heart grew cold."

William found Rosedale too large for himself alone, and decided to rent it. It was, however, impossible to find a tenant for the large, sprawling house and he decided to divide it into two houses. He writes Fanny in April 1854 that he is "keeping the house, lawn, and the portion of ground encircled by the road leading to what was the stables, and so round to the fence and to a certain distance below the brow of the hill. This embraces forty-one acres and has been reserved from the sale to Mr. Carruthers and for the remainder, he is to pay £12,500 in the place of £15,000 for the whole. . . . I intend to put the house in thorough repair and erect a stable and coach house on the northeast corner of the portion retained and put a substantial fence around it and, if a good tenant offers, to let it for two years. . . ."

In the following October the Sheriff, who had always spoiled his eldest daughter, writes again to Fanny, "Most assuredly you shall have Rosedale as a residence, if you desire it. I had taken the notice from the paper the moment you expressed a desire respecting it. . . ."

Fanny (Mrs. Meredith) writes in her *Recollections*, "My sister Louisa and Augustus Nanton were married 4th May [1855] and when they returned from their honeymoon, they shared dear old Rosedale house, or rather half of it, with me, Professor and Mrs. Kingston and their two children living in the other half."

The Kingstons did not stay long and Fanny's sister Sarah, who had married Lieutenant Lewis Ord, moved into that half of the house. Mary's three daughters were now all living again in Rosedale. They continued to share the house for some years, and a number of Jarvis grandchildren were born there.

The last great event at Rosedale was the garden party of October 1861, on the occasion of the distribution of prize money won by the militia in a rifle match, and it was also the last reunion of the veterans of the War of 1812.

William Botsford Jarvis died at Rosedale in July 1864. His daughters continued to share Rosedale, but when Edmund Meredith's government position required residence in Ottawa, they decided to rent the house.

The caption in *The Toronto Illustrated News* read: "Garden party on Sheriff Jarvis's lawn, Rosedale, Toronto, October 23, 1861, showing many survivors of the War of 1812, and General Williams, Hero of Kars."

— Ontario Archives

Finally, when the remaining land was subdivided and sold, Sir David Macpherson of nearby Chestnut Park bought what was called the "Rosedale Homestead." His daughter, Christina, and her husband, Percival F. Ridout, lived there from 1889 until 1905. Its address was now 12 Rosedale Road.

In 1905, the old house (about where 30 Rosedale Road is now) was demolished, and gradually the neighbourhood changed. Many wild flowers and old trees disappeared; the ravine was filled in, and the rushing stream now runs through a sewer.

Today a small apartment house stands on the site of Mary's Rosedale, and a number of solid houses of no particular distinction occupy the fields where Sheriff Jarvis once pastured his cows.

The front of beautiful Holland House appeared to have been lifted from a much earlier century. It was more like a medieval fortress castle than the respectable home of Solicitor General Henry Boulton. The fountain is in the Queen's Hotel grounds.

— Mrs. H.P. Wright

Holland House

1831-1904

Holland House was one of the most romantic of early York houses. It was often called "The Castle" — because it looked like one.

Henry John Boulton, whose castle it was, was born in 1790 in the famous London Holland House, which his father had rented from Lord Holland. He was taken to York when his father moved there in 1797. As a youth he was something of a dandy, as shown in a letter written in 1808 to John Macaulay: ". . . I met young Henry Boulton with his father and mother, all on horseback, on their way from York to Cornwall. He is quite a beau, booted and spurred, with a pin in his cravat that comes even with his nose. . . ."

Henry was sent to England to finish his education, and was called to the English Bar in 1815. In 1816 he returned to Upper Canada and began to practise law. (He was Samuel Peter Jarvis's second in the famous 1817 duel, when John Ridout was killed.)

In 1818 Henry became Solicitor General, and the same year he married Eliza Jones, the daughter of a Loyalist. It was at this time that Henry's older brother, D'Arcy, was building The Grange, where portraits of Henry and Eliza still hang today.

In 1820 Henry bought a town lot in York from his father, on the south side of Market Street (Wellington), between Bay and York Streets. This lot was one acre in area, about 210 feet wide and 210 feet deep. In 1827 he bought an acre lot on the north side of Front Street, south of his Wellington Street lot.

Henry became Attorney General of the province in 1829. The following year he was elected to the Legislative Assembly for Niagara, where he led a strong group of Tory members. He was prospering, and decided to build a suitable home for his growing family.

In 1831 he built a notable house near the north end of his Wellington Street lot on the site of a wooden house, formerly occupied by his father. He called it "Holland House" in memory of his birthplace. The house faced south to Front Street and the lake, and the south lot was intended as lawn and gardens. The main approach to Holland House was from Front Street by a drive which wound to the front of the house, and then to the stables in the rear on the west side. The 1833 York Directory gave the address as "50 Front Street, an elegant newly erected Gothic mansion, stucco'd." The same directory listed it on Wellington Street as "Backfront of the splendid mansion of H.J. Boulton Esq."

The garden front of Holland House appeared to have been lifted from a much earlier century. Resembling a medieval fortress castle, the central part was a wide, circular tower, three storeys high, with a crenelated roof, large Gothic windows at the second floor level, and small narrow openings on the third floor. Three large arches on the ground floor of this baronial tower led to the front entrance. Massive chimneys near the four corners of the roof were disguised in round turrets, and a battlemented parapet ran around the flat roof of the entire building. A projecting portico at second-floor level provided a narrow gallery, where the occupants could walk and view the scene to the south, and, if necessary, pour boiling lead on attackers. The visual effect from Front Street or the Bay was startling and bizarre in colonial York. One almost expected to see a moat and drawbridge guarded by knights in armour, or at least a portcullis.

There was a certain schizophrenia about Holland House, not only because it appeared to have two fronts and no rear, but its two fronts were so completely different they might have belonged to two distinct buildings.

The Honourable Henry Boulton did not enjoy his castle, Holland House, for very long. In 1833 he was dismissed from his post as Attorney General and sent to Newfoundland.

— Art Gallery of Ontario

The Wellington Street front, flanked by a low wing on each side, was plain, with little claim to distinction. The entrance was at the extreme left, through a square porch. A high archway at the west side led to large brick stables. Built of brick, covered by stucco outlined to resemble brown stone, the house was set close to the street and guarded by a wrought-iron fence. In later years when Henry sold the Front Street lot, the main carriage entrance to Holland House was from Wellington Street, and the original "backfront" became the "front front"; the address from 1846 on was "Wellington Street west of Bay Street." Later still it was 61 Wellington Street.

Henry did not enjoy his castle for very long. In 1833 he was in hot water for a daring speech he had made in the Legislative Assembly. He had attacked the Colonial Office for its reception of William Lyon Mackenzie in Westminster the preceding year and he was summarily dismissed. He went to London to explain matters, but found it impossible to be re-instated, although he was somewhat consoled by being appointed Chief Justice of Newfoundland.

When he left for his new post, Henry did not sell Holland House, as he hoped eventually to return to Upper Canada. He rented it. The first tenant was Captain John Elmsley, who lived there briefly while his home, Clover Hill, was being completed. In 1837 John G. Howard, the architect busy finishing his own Colborne Lodge in High Park, wrote in his journal, "Made great repairs at Holland House for Captain Truscott, Manager of the Farmers' Agricultural Bank on King St., which afterwards failed."

In 1838 Henry John Boulton was again in trouble. He was dismissed from his office as Chief Justice of Newfoundland for meddling in local politics. He returned to Toronto, and the family once more occupied their castle. Henry resumed his law practice, and, following the Union of the Canadas in 1841, he represented Niagara in the Legislative Assembly for three years. Appointed to the Executive Council of the Province of Canada, he was also mayor of Toronto from 1846 to 1849 and sat for Norfolk in the Assembly from 1848 to 1851. He was a director of the Bank of Upper Canada and lived at Holland House until his death in June 1870. Eliza had died there in 1868.

Although Henry and Eliza had many children, a number of them died in infancy but five daughters lived to maturity and were all married in splendid style at Holland House. In 1843 Harriet Eliza, the eldest, married Clarke Gamble, a successful barrister. Sophia, the second daughter, married Colonel James Forlong of Gore Vale. Elizabeth married John Hillyard Cameron of The Meadows, but died in 1844 aged twenty one. Clara Louisa married a John Cayley, and Charlotte Augusta, the youngest daughter, married William H. Crawford of Quebec.

Their eldest son, William Henry Forster, died in infancy; Charles Knightley, born in 1827, died at the age of nineteen when thrown from a horse; Henry John married in England in 1852; George D'Arcy, the youngest son, was born in Newfoundland, and he married Juliana, eldest daughter of Thomas Gibbs Ridout, and took a prominent part in Toronto politics.

In 1850 Clarke Gamble and Harriet Eliza moved into Holland House and shared it with the Boultons for several years. Since the rooms were large and well proportioned, the families do not appear to have been crowded. In 1865 Gamble and his family returned to Holland House and stayed there until he built his own mansion, Pinehurst, east of The Grange.

After Henry died Holland House was bought by Alexander Manning, a wealthy Irish contractor. He owned the Grand Opera House, built the Manning Arcade and Manning Chambers, was mayor of Toronto between 1873 and 1875, and president of both the North American Land Company and the Toronto Brewing and Malting Company. The Mannings completely renovated Holland House and furnished it in sumptuous style.

For some years a row of four houses on the north side of Front Street, south and slightly west of Holland House, had been a hotel. At one time the row had been Knox College, then Sword's Hotel. In the 1860s it was greatly enlarged and became the Queen's Hotel, the most elegant in the province. Only a board fence separated the gardens of the Queen's Hotel (on the site of today's Royal York Hotel) from the grounds of Holland House where the Mannings had an unobstructed view of the hotel grounds with its splendid fountain, and could observe the guests playing croquet on the lawns or taking tea in fine weather.

On one occasion, the tower gallery of Holland House provided ringside seats for a travelling circus being held in the grounds of the Queen's.

During the 1880s the Queen's Hotel was at the height of its glory, boasting an elevator, central heat, and running water in the bedrooms. European royalty, celebrated actors and musicians, and prominent politicians stayed there.

In 1872 when Governor General Lord Dufferin visited Toronto, the Manning family vacated Holland House and placed it at his disposal. The arrangement demonstrates the high opinion in which the stately house was held. During the vice regal occupancy, a number of elaborate entertainments were held there.

The Mannings lived in Holland House until 1887. They then moved to Queen's Park because their daughter Blanche had died at Holland House, and the house had too many sad memories.

It was proposed that the dignified castle be purchased for use as a Government House, but nothing came of this suggestion. The Ontario Reform Association rented it and its grounds, made some alterations, and used it as its headquarters and clubhouse. One wonders what ultra-Tory Henry Boulton would have thought of his home becoming the Reform Club!

Between 1891 and 1892 it stood empty. Then William Miller, a painter, occupied it briefly but it was soon empty again.

The lovely gardens and trees south of the house were disappearing, and a narrow lane called Piper Street bisected the block between Wellington and Front Streets. A gravel walk from this lane led to the south door, but there was no longer the fine view of the Bay.

In a neighbourhood no longer fashionable as a residential area, the old castle was impractical. Warehouses and commercial establishments were appearing on Wellington Street, and Holland House remained without tenant or buyer, occupied only by a resident caretaker.

The great fire of 1904 destroyed an adjacent building but spared Holland House. A few months later, however, picturesque Holland House, an anachronism in twentieth century downtown Toronto, was razed to the ground.

Drumsnab
1834-

Drumsnab is believed to be the oldest house in Toronto continuously occupied as a private home. Its address today is 5 Drumsnab Road, just north of the Castle Frank subway station. The site was originally part of a 200-acre lot granted in 1796 by the Crown to Captain George Playter, a Quaker Loyalist. The lot was north of the 2nd Concession (Bloor Street) and east from Yonge Street to the Don River. Playter also acquired land at the north end of the Castle Frank property, to the south of the concession line. His house was about where 2 Castle Frank Crescent stands now; his lodgehouse was at the head of modern Parliament Street.

The western part of Playter's land became the Jarvis's estate, Rosedale, and in 1834 Francis Cayley bought 118 acres from Playter on the east side for £1,525. Francis, born in 1809, was the descendant of a Norman who had accompanied William the Conqueror to England.

He built a solid, one-storey house north of Playter's and called it "Drumsnab," from a house in a Scott novel. Drumsnab, the north country word for sugarloaf, was suggested by the round-topped hill across the ravine to the east of the house locally known as the "Sugar Loaf." In October 1793 Mrs. Simcoe mentioned in her diary the steep "sugar-loafed hills" beside the upper Don River. Refined sugar was at that time bought by householders in conical loaves and cut into lumps with sugar nippers.

Drumsnab, high above the ravines, had a superb vista of the Don Valley and the river, then clear and fast-running. Isolated in wild surroundings, it was a charming Regency cottage built of fieldstone taken from the property. The deep foundations were thirty inches thick, the stone walls and inner partitions two feet thick, covered with roughcast on the outside and plastered directly on the stone inside. Not a single nail was used in the studding, and the fine wood for floors, door and window-frames, wainscot, and balusters came from giant trees on the estate.

The house faced south. It was nearly square, with a gently sloping roof, four sturdy chimneys, and a wide verandah around all but the north side. The rooms were spacious, with twelve-foot-high ceilings. Long windows, with folding inner shutters, opened to the verandah. The front entrance hall was forty-five feet long with a large fireplace. It

Drumsnab is probably the oldest house in Toronto continuously occupied as a private home. It is a charming Regency cottage built of fieldstone taken from the property and has a superb view of the Don Valley.
— Ellen Russell

was lighted by a window back of the stairs and one at the landing, both nearly ten feet high with semicircular tops.

Francis Cayley was literary, artistic, and whimsical. He painted unusual frescoes — in the hall a floor-to-ceiling hatrack with his hat, cloak, and walking stick. He wrote beneath it, "As long as Drumsnab stands my hat and cloak will hang in the front hall." Later owners covered the walls with wallpaper. What a surprise when the present owners restored the house and the forgotten fresco was revealed!

Francis painted the drawing room walls with scenes from Goethe's *Faust*, the door panels with Don Quixote characters, and the Cayley coat of arms above the door, illustrating the motto, "When the cat's away the mice will play," with a mouse orchestra on one side of the shield and a cat on the other side.

In its early years the vast basement was the practical centre of the house. The huge kitchen in the northwest corner, where all cooking was done in the fireplace, had pine floors; the large buttery or cool room under the drawing room had a brick floor.

In 1847 Francis's younger brother John married Clara Boulton of Holland House. Soon afterwards they moved in with bachelor Francis. In 1850 they decided to add a second storey. Evidence suggests that the roof was jacked up, the second floor and attic built, and the roof lowered again. The dining room bay was carried up to the roof, which projects above it in a pleasing curve. The addition, with brick walls and thirteen-foot ceilings, contained a ballroom across the entire south side and several bedrooms with immense windows. The third floor contained servants' rooms and storerooms. The house now had eleven fireplaces; those on the second floor with marble mantels in the new style in contrast to the wooden mantels of the ground floor.

Francis died in 1874 and John sold Drumsnab and its thirty-five acres to Maunsell B. Jackson, K.C., for $15,750. The Jacksons rebuilt the verandah, adding a balcony, and installed gas, a furnace, and a ground-floor kitchen. Maunsell Jr. was born and died there eighty-eight years later, while his sister, Mrs. R.S. Morley, lived there for ninety years. It was during this period that most of the land around Drumsnab was sold.

In 1914 the Prince Edward Viaduct was built joining Bloor Street and Danforth Avenue. A piece of the south side of Drumsnab and a half acre of ravine were expropriated, and the picturesque lodgehouse built by Playter in 1818, which Francis Cayley had used as a studio, was demolished.

In 1961 Drumsnab lost a slice on its east side when the Don Valley Parkway opened. The sugar-loaf hill which gave the house its name disappeared, and the house is now perched close to the raw edge of the hill. The once superb view of the Don River has been replaced by a view of a six-lane freeway.

In 1965 John Morley, Mrs. R.S. Morley's son, sold Drumsnab to M.F. Feheley of T.D.F. Artists Ltd. The house was in poor repair and the Feheleys embarked on a careful restoration project. They retained Drumsnab's nineteenth century character, but added modern comforts.

The hallway of Drumsnab, looking slightly dilapidated, before the present owners renovated it.

— Jack Mitchell

The worn pine floor of the front hall has been replaced by large squares of black and white marble, and the hall door to the dining room is closed up. The drawing room frescoes were so grimy that they have been covered with wallpaper, except for two on a door. The carved plaster ceiling medallion, still fitted for a gas fixture, has been cleaned and is again very handsome.

The Morleys had used the downstairs bedroom as a chopping room to cut fireplace wood and this scarred room is now restored as a library. In the basement when bricks and plumbing were removed, the original bake oven was discovered.

Drumsnab, its stucco today a delicate pink, has begun a new life and the large rooms are a splendid setting for what is probably the finest collection of Eskimo sculpture in the world.

Colborne Lodge in 1903 — a delightful Regency style country house with an old fashioned English garden and flowering vines swarming over the verandah.

— Charles Abel Photos

Colborne Lodge
1836-

John George Howard was an engineer, surveyor, artist, and architect. Born near London, England, in 1803, he was sent to sea at fourteen. There he learned navigation, marine surveying, and practical geometry. At sixteen he entered the office of a London architect.

In 1827 John married Jemima Meikle, daughter of a prosperous Scot. Times were hard in the Scotland of 1832 and they decided to follow Jemima's sister Fanny and her husband to Goderich in Upper Canada. After three months of incredible adventures — shipwreck, mutiny, and a cholera epidemic — they reached York.

Walking up Church Street, John saw in a pawnbroker's window the carving set he and Jemima had given Fanny as a wedding gift. He bought the carving set, helped poverty stricken Fanny and her family, and decided to stay in York.

After a wretched winter, John met the Lieutenant Governor, Sir John Colborne, who was looking for a drawing master for Upper Canada College. John submitted sketches of various buildings and won first prize from among six other entrants. He got the job. It paid £100 a year for four mornings a week, leaving afternoons free for private practice.

Everyone was speculating in land and erecting buildings. York needed an architect and soon John had all the work he could handle.

In 1834, when York became the city of Toronto, Mayor Mackenzie appointed him City Surveyor, and in spite of long skirts and rough terrain, Jemima helped John run the lines and sketched prospective buildings.

John laid the first plank sidewalks in the city on King Street, built two lodges at the Queen Street entrance to modern University Avenue, stores, offices and private villas, and designed everything from the King Street sewer to stables and tennis courts. He won £45 for his design for the Toronto Court House and Gaol.

In 1836 he bought a piece of land on the east side of the Humber River, fronting a deep indentation of Lake Ontario. It was Lot 37. It extended to modern Bloor Street and contained 165 acres. (Lots 36, 37, and 38 had been granted by the Crown to King's College, which sold them at £1 per acre.)

John planned to farm his lot, but first he built his home on a high promontory facing the Bay. He called it "Colborne Lodge" in honour of the man whose patronage had launched his career. Some years later he bought a full length portrait of Colborne (then Lord Seton) and hung it in Colborne Lodge.

Progress on the house was slow — the roads over which materials had to be hauled were bad, and John had little time to devote to his own building. When Colborne Lodge was almost ready, the Rebellion erupted, and on December 7, 1837, Howard led one wing of the scouting party of loyal townsmen up Yonge Street to fight Mackenzie and his rebels. John acquitted himself so well he was commissioned a lieutenant in the militia.

On December 23 the Howards moved into Colborne Lodge. His journal records that he shot a deer on Christmas Day, and the next day a bald-headed eagle with a seven-foot wing spread, which he stuffed.

Colborne Lodge was a country home, simple but comfortable. John was familiar with the Regency style popular for suburban villas which was replacing the restrained Loyalist style. He chose the new, more picturesque design, but omitted dormer windows and some other details.

Originally Colborne Lodge was a modest stucco rectangle with a wide, three-sided bay jutting from the drawing room facing the lake. A shallow verandah with an awning-roof, supported by slender wooden columns in true Regency fashion, but without the treillage, stretched across the south side.

John Howard at eighty, and Jemima Howard. When John was first appointed City Surveyor in 1834, Jemima helped him run the lines, despite Toronto's rough terrain and her long skirts. — Metropolitan Toronto Library Board

The front door is not as impressive as front doors in earlier gentlemen's houses. It opens to a small vestibule leading to a square hall, which has a window to the verandah on the right and two doors opposite the front door. The rooms lead one from another in a semicircular arrangment around a central core of fireplaces. To the right is the drawing room, a pleasant, rather small room with three French windows in the bay opening to the verandah. The wooden mantelpiece is painted to resemble veined cream marble, carved in classical style.

The basement looks unchanged. The original kitchen, with brick floor and bake oven beside the huge brick fireplace, is reached by a steep, narrow staircase and wider outside steps. The basement bedrooms, one with a fireplace, were for servants and were probably more comfortable in winter than the family bedrooms exposed to the bitter wind from the lake. The master bedroom has small, high windows above the verandah roof, suggesting that originally Colborne Lodge may have been only one-and-a-half storeys. An interesting "dumb" stove, a tall iron cylinder with a stovepipe through the ceiling, carried heat from a stove set up below in winter. It looks like a stove, but has no fire-box or lid. Two narrow spare rooms, each with a single bed, were frequently used by Jemima's nieces.

Soon after moving in John bought Lot 35 of 160 acres immediately east of Colborne Lodge for £257. On it he planned to build a few houses and gradually sell them. He called one house "Sunnyside"; eventually the whole area became known as Sunnyside.

At the rear of the original Colborne Lodge is a large, two-storey wing, added about 1865. The ground floor contains the new kitchen, which is down four steps from the large pantry, next to the dining room. It must have been a great pleasure to the servants when a huge wood-and-coal range replaced fireplace cooking and baking. Also, four wide steps to the dining room were a great improvement over the narrow, twisting stairway from the basement for carrying heavy trays. Further modern improvements were a small, indoor pump and iron sink and large cupboards to the ceiling. Shortly afterwards a furnace was installed.

One of the most interesting rooms at Colborne Lodge is the bathroom, said to be the first in Toronto with running water — then a novelty. It is on the ground floor in the new wing. The taps for the bathtub are on the wall beside it, linked to a tank in the room above. Water was heated by an ingenious connection with a stove there, but the tank had to be filled with water carried upstairs in pails.

The large bedroom above the new kitchen became Jemima's room. In the last years of her life Jemima was ill and was constantly attended by a nurse. Howard's letters refer to the "hole in her breast," which in the final years became so painful it drove her out of her mind.

Attached to the ground-floor kitchen is the conservatory, which John called his "glass house." The floor is brick, and a staircase leads down to the old kitchen in the basement. The master of Colborne Lodge was keenly interested in horticulture, always experimenting to develop new and hardier specimens.

As the years passed, John became increasingly busy. As both surveyor and engineer for the city, he surveyed Toronto Harbour, laid out

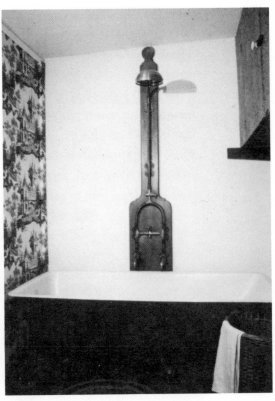

Above left: A dumb stove in a bedroom in Colborne Lodge. Above right: The bathroom in Colborne Lodge was the first in Toronto with running water.

— Toronto Historical Board

streets and sidewalks, built sewers and bridges, and frequently acted as arbitrator in disputes, especially following the all-too-frequent fires. He won the competition to build the lunatic asylum on Queen Street, the largest of all his works, which occupied him during most of the 1840s. He made alterations to Government House, adding a new ballroom, and in 1843 he designed Brock's Monument at Queenston Heights, later to be blown up by Irish Americans. In his private practice he designed banks, breweries, theatres, houses, and St. James' Cemetery. In many Ontario towns, the schools, churches, markets, courthouses, and jails first appeared on John Howard's drawing board. There was nothing he would not attempt.

His land was the highest in the area, so he called it "High Park." He was too busy to farm it himself, so in 1851 he built a farmhouse and barn and installed a farmer, who continued clearing the forest. Despite the many shallow ravines, the farmer managed to plant forty acres of wheat and seventy-five of clover. He also made hundreds of fence posts.

In 1856 John retired from his position at Upper Canada College and resigned his surveying and engineering posts. He had been on the Committee of the first Artists' Society in Toronto in 1834, and in 1847 he became Treasurer and Vice President of the Toronto Society of Arts. Both he and Jemima spent their leisure hours painting. A barn-like building near the house with a large skylight was their studio and art gallery. When he died it contained many watercolours of Toronto and High Park scenes, in addition to other subjects. Aside from their artistic merit, these pictures are valuable illustrations of early buildings and landscapes, long since vanished.

The grounds of Colborne Lodge were beautiful. A profusion of flowers in an old fashioned English garden and flowering vines swarming over the verandah created a delightful air of informality. Three long-tailed serpents, with glaring eyes and fiery tongues, guarded the house and acted as railings to the verandah. They were, in fact, long, twisted cedar roots which Howard had carved and painted until they looked startlingly real. Today, only one of these alarming dragons remains.

Mounted on a spur of land in front of the house was a large brass navy gun. John fired the gun every day at sunrise and sunset, with a special salvo on the Queen's birthday and important family occasions.

Near this old cannon, which is still in place, was a large beacon light, set on a carved three-legged stand. At dusk every evening Howard lighted this lantern to aid small boats returning from the Humber River. He extinguished it at precisely midnight. A sketch made in 1935 shows the beacon still in front of Colborne Lodge, but it has since disappeared.

He carved several graceful white swans, which he set in front of the house. One of these, on a low column, appears in a 1928 etching. At one time a sundial stood on a square table in front of the house. This was later removed to City Hall, and one wonders whose garden it now graces.

Howard loved birds and enjoyed carving, with the result that many unusual birdhouses were scattered among the trees of High Park. He also carved an exact model of the park.

In 1873 the Howards, who had no children, decided to give High Park to the City of Toronto. They proposed to give 120 acres at once, for use as a public park, retaining Colborne Lodge and 45 acres until their deaths, when it, too, would pass to the city. There were two strings attached: one, the city must pay John a pension of $1,200 a year until his death, and, two, promise that no intoxicating beverage would ever be sold in High Park. Although John was seventy years old at the time, the cautious council did not agree immediately, feeling that $1,200 a year, for an indeterminate number of years, might prove costly. After debating for six weeks, during which John pointed out that the house and grounds were worth at least $24,000 and that he would act as caretaker, they decided to gamble and agreed to the deal.

In 1876 Howard was appointed Forest Ranger of High Park at a salary of one dollar a year. During his last years he greatly improved the park, building roads and drains, and clearing the underbush. He designed ornamental entrance gates, bridges, and pavilions. He also erected a small station on the lakeshore for women and children waiting for the trains which now ran between Colborne Lodge and the Bay.

In 1877 Jemima died and was interred in the tomb built two years previously, a short distance southwest of Colborne Lodge. The memorial cairn, of large granite boulders, is a tribute to Jemima's Scottish blood, and the large Maltese Cross, which surmounts the cairn, reflects Howard's allegiance to the Knights Templar Order. The cairn is guarded by a handsome wrought-iron fence, designed in 1714 by Sir Christopher Wren. The fence surrounded St. Paul's Cathedral in London for many years. When it was removed from St. Paul's in 1874, John bought it to enclose his house and garden, but the ship which carried it went aground near Montreal and only a small part of the fence was salvaged.

In 1890 John died, having been nearly blind for several years. He was interred in the vault he had prepared. The deed which conveyed High Park to Toronto stipulated that his land always be called High Park — which answers those who feel it should be called Howard Park.

The deed stated that it was to be "kept select for the wives and children of the mechanics and the working classes generally, also the Sunday school children, and the different charities' picnics." The city agreed that "no drinking-booth, alehouse, saloon, or tavern" would ever be allowed in the park, and no intoxicating drinks were ever to be sold there.

Howard's pension had been paid for seventeen years. It amounted to a total of $20,400 in addition to his salary of $17 as Park Ranger. The total was not far from the valuation he had placed on the property in 1873, but there were some who grumbled that Howard's noble gift had been too costly. They seemed to think he had swindled them by surviving to the age of eighty-seven.

For more than thirty years Colborne Lodge remained vacant and neglected, pillaged by souvenir hunters and suffering from the elements. Eventually it became so decayed city officials could think of no other solution but to demolish it. Then the Women's Canadian Historical Society, Toronto Branch, came to the rescue. In 1925 they persuaded city officials to grant them $4,000 to clean and repair the ruin. The sum was barely enough to keep the body and soul of the house together, but by dint of almost superhuman effort they were able, in November 1927, to hand over the key of Colborne Lodge to Mayor McBride. The city had made some needed repairs to the exterior and had closed the old well beneath the basement kitchen, but the beautifully restored house was the result of much hard work and patient research on the part of the Society.

In the drawing room the pale blue and green damask covering the mahogany furniture is a replica of the original covers. The oil portraits of John and Jemima, painted by Thomas Stevenson in 1848, hang on the walls where they have always hung. The feather flowers made by Jemima and the birds stuffed by John are once more on the mantel.

The original Howard homestead of 165 acres is the central part of High Park. Subsequently, more land was bought by the city from the Ridout estate on the east and the Chapman (formerly Ellis) estate on the west. High Park now contains slightly more than four hundred acres, and it is larger than Hyde Park in London, but only half the size of Central Park in New York.

Lyndhurst
1837-1961

Front Street has changed much over the last century and a half. Where the *Globe and Mail* is now published once stood the modest home of Robert Sympson Jameson and his famous wife Anna. The house was then beside Lake Ontario.

Anna Murphy was born in Dublin in 1794, the daughter of a struggling artist. She married the English barrister Jameson in 1826. They were ill-matched, attracted only by a mutual interest in art and literature. Robert was reserved, with a cold manner; Anna was a traveller and gifted writer, involved in the lives of everyone around her. They soon separated.

In 1833 Jameson was appointed Attorney General of Upper Canada. He bought a piece of land on the outskirts of Toronto on Front Street, west of Brock Street, as Spadina Avenue south of Queen Street was then called.

He wrote Anna, "I have been fencing in my nice little piece of ground on the banks of the lake where I am promising myself the happiness of building you a pretty little villa after your own taste. I have set a man to plant some trees and shrubs also, for the place was quite denuded, though by far the finest situation in town. I have ground enough for a pretty, extensive garden, nearly three acres."

Early in 1835 he wrote again: "My hopes of receiving you in a house of your own have been thwarted. I have not the requisite money but I have the ground and before long I trust to have a nice cottage on it."

He urges her to join him. In October 1836 Anna set sail for Canada. She landed in New York and set off for Toronto. The journey took eight days by paddle-wheeler up the Hudson, carriage to Albany, railroad to Utica, stagecoach to Rochester, hired carriage to Lewiston, ferryboat across the Niagara River to Queenston, spring-cart to Niagara, and, finally, a steamer across Lake Ontario. She arrived exhausted in mid-December, walked through ankle-deep slush to Jameson's rooms on Brock Street, and found nothing prepared for her. This first impression left her with a permanently jaundiced view of Toronto. Her description has been frequently quoted: "A little ill-built town on low land at the bottom of a frozen bay, with one very ugly church without tower or steeple, some Government offices built of staring red brick in the most tasteless, vulgar style imaginable, three feet of snow all round — I did not expect much, but for this I was not prepared."

"The new house which he is building from the plans I have seen must be a nice, comfortable little place. I remarked that there was no arrangement made for any friend who might stray this way, but I thought the omission characteristic," she wrote her family.

In February 1837 Jameson was appointed Vice-Chancellor of Upper Canada with an increase in income. Anna now believed he had urged her to join him mainly for appearances. "No one loves him but everyone approves him, and the moving into his new residence will occupy Mr. Jameson and me for a month or two," she wrote.

And in March: "About a week ago we moved into a new house — it is not quite finished. It will be very pretty and pleasant no doubt when it is not so cold and comfortless. We are surrounded by a garden of some extent, or what will be a garden — we are so completely blockaded by ice and mud that to reach the door is a matter of some difficulty and even danger. Planks laid from one snowheap to another form the only access. The site, though now so dreary, must be charming in summer for we command at one glance the entrance to the Bay, the King's Pier, the light-house, and the whole expanse of the lake to the Niagara shore."

Soon afterwards Anna wrote her sister Charlotte: "The house is very pretty and compact — but I take no pleasure in anything. The place, the society are so detestable to me, my own domestic position so painful that to remain here would be death to me. . . ."

Anna Jameson, author of *Winter Studies and Summer Rambles*, and her husband, Robert Jameson. She thoroughly disliked Toronto and found its society "fourth rate and half educated."

— Ontario Archives

— Metropolitan Toronto Library Board

The house was small and unpretentious, with the entrance on Wellington Place. Built of brick, it was a square block of two storeys and a small one-storey wing on each side, with large windows and a verandah across the rear. It was in the centre of the property and its best feature was the view from the south side over the lake.

Anna's opinion of Toronto society was unflattering. "I am in a community of fourth-rate, half-educated or uneducated people, where local politics of the meanest kind engross the men and petty gossip and household cares the women." She had been accustomed to mingling on equal terms with famous writers and artists and had been lionized as an art authority, but in Toronto she was merely the wife of the important Vice-Chancellor.

Meanwhile, she continued writing and sketching, although "my fingers are so frozen I can scarcely write." She complained that she had only three servants, all quite unsatisfactory.

Anna visited Niagara Falls, and in the spring she set out to explore as far as Detroit, spending a week with the eccentric Colonel Talbot on Lake Erie. She went with the Indian agent by canoe to Lake Huron, Manitoulin Island, and Lake Simcoe, the only white woman at the gift ceremonies. Her unheard-of travels led to *Winter Studies and Summer Rambles*, in three volumes. The modern version omits her tiresome moralizing and has become a Canadian classic.

In September 1837 Anna left Toronto and never returned. She continued to write learned books which brought her prestige but little money. Jameson sent her a small allowance but no letters. She heard he was drinking heavily.

He bought large tracts of land west of his house along the lakefront (Jameson Avenue in Parkdale is on this land). In 1849, although only fifty-one years old, he was retired on a pension of £750 a year. Anna was told that she would receive no further allowance but would inherit the land. This came as a blow, because she was supporting her mother and sisters and desperately needed the money.

In 1844 Jameson sold the house to Frederick Widder for £2,000. In 1854 he died. His will read, ". . . I bequeath all my property to my good friends George and Emma Maynard . . . my personal property the same. . . ." Anna had never heard of the Maynards, with whom he had been living.

Frederick Widder, Chief Commissioner of the Canada Company, was born in London, England, in 1801 and was proud of his family connection with Austro-Bavarian royalty. His English home was called "Lyndhurst," and he immediately named his new house "Lyndhurst."

The Widders greatly enlarged the house. They added a wing on the west side and two storeys above the whole house. The result was a massive, four-storey building with a mansard roof and a tower at the southwest corner. A large ballroom was an important feature.

The floors were uneven where the new and old portions joined, but ornate columns concealed it. The new double drawing room was splendid — white marble mantels, long windows, and crystal chandeliers. It had a decorative cornice and a much higher ceiling than Anna's little parlour.

Above: The Lyndhurst drawing room in the 1860s during the Widders' occupancy.
Below: The same drawing room at the turn of the century after Lyndhurst had
become Loretto Abbey.   — Metropolitan Toronto Library Board
                                                  — Panda Associates

A large stained-glass window was installed in the front hall with the family crest showing a ram on an azure field — *Widder* being German for ram.

For twenty years Lyndhurst was the scene of glittering social events. Balls, dinner parties, and many smart affairs were held here. Every visiting European notable was entertained, and in summer delightful garden parties were held on the lawn near the lake.

Elizabeth Widder also had royal connections. Her father, Sir Henry Moore, was distantly related to the British royal family. A rivalry developed between Mrs. Widder and Mrs. William Proudfoot of Kearsney House on Dundonald Street. Mrs. Proudfoot was the leader of the dignified element, while Mrs. Widder led the sprightly set. Mrs. Proudfoot gave sedate card parties; Mrs. Widder elegant musical evenings. After dinner at Lyndhurst, the gentlemen often gathered around Mrs. Widder at the piano and sang rollicking French voyageur songs. At Lyndhurst charades and fancy dress parties amused guests. At Kearsney House balls, stately quadrilles predominated, while lively gallops, mazurkas, and polkas were enjoyed at Lyndhurst.

In summer the Widders gave boating parties and held archery contests on the lawn. This sport, one of the few in which ladies could take an active part, was extremely popular until Lady Head introduced croquet. Then it became the rage.

The most brilliant affair at Lyndhurst was the private ball for the Prince of Wales, later Edward VII, when he visited Toronto in September 1860.

In 1865 Widder retired. Shortly afterwards both he and Mrs. Widder died and Lyndhurst was put up for auction. With its splendid appointments, the big house, now in a fashionable area on the lakeshore, was expected to be eagerly sought, but there was only one person who wanted it. A Mr. Gordon thought he had it. In May 1866 he went to England to talk to the holders of the large mortgage, and his wife and family even moved into Lyndhurst under a sort of lease, but no action was taken on the bid. By this time railroads were beginning to mar the lakeshore and roundhouses had already appeared near Spadina Avenue.

In March 1867 the Sisters of Loretto started negotiating for Lyndhurst. The house and three and a half acres of land were bought for

$70,000. Gordon, far from Toronto, was unable to prevent the sale. Mrs. Gordon refused to allow the nuns to view the house, but they took possession in September anyway.

Lyndhurst became the mother house of Loretto Abbey and a "School for Young Ladies." An 1870 advertisement reads: "Loretto Abbey, a spacious and splendid mansion situated conveniently near the business part of the city, yet sufficiently remote to secure the quiet and seclusion necessary for study. It combines the advantages of the city with those of the country, having the full benefit of the pure air of the lake. The course of Instruction comprises every branch suitable to the Education of Young Ladies with especial attention to impart elegance and lady-like deportment. For Board and Tuition $100 per annum, Wellington Place, Toronto."

Loretto Abbey made numerous additions to Lyndhurst to provide music rooms, dormitories, and other rooms essential to a large convent and boarding school. One five-storey wing contained a beautiful chapel surmounted by a large dome. For sixty-three years Loretto Abbey flourished in old Lyndhurst. Central heating was introduced, and elaborately covered radiators appeared in rooms still dominated by fireplaces.

Eventually the building became black with soot from the new factories, the once pure air was polluted by cinders from trains, and the lovely view vanished as the lake was pushed back.

In 1930 The Society of Jesus purchased the buildings and Loretto Abbey moved to Armour Heights. Further additions were built to accommodate a large seminary. In 1959 the property was bought by The Telegram Publishing Company and the Jesuits moved to Bayview Avenue. In 1961 Lyndhurst was demolished. A modern publishing complex, facing Front Street, was erected on the site.

Early in 1974 *The Globe and Mail* moved into the complex, which it had bought when *The Evening Telegram* ceased publication in 1971.

Where Chancellor Jameson planted trees in a garden beside the lake are now ugly railroad tracks; where ladies in sweeping skirts enjoyed archery and croquet, factories have replaced lawns; the unhappy Jameson house and splendid Lyndhurst are both forgotten.

Wykeham Hall

1841-1929

For many years a picturesque house stood in what is now another construction site, but was until recently the parking lot of Eaton's College Street store. James Buchanan Macaulay built it about 1841 and gave it the name of "Wickham Lodge," after the village of Wickham in Hampshire, England, where Macaulay's relatives still lived.

James Buchanan Macaulay was born in 1793 in Niagara. He was the son of Dr. James Macaulay and Elizabeth Hayter, and grew up in his parents' home, Teraulay Cottage, now the site of Holy Trinity Church. Following an active part in the War of 1812 as an officer in the Glengarry Fencibles, he became a law student. In 1821 he married Rachel Gamble and they had one son and four daughters. After James had practised law for seven years, in 1829 he was appointed a puisne judge in the Court of Queen's Bench.

Judge Macaulay had inherited a ten-acre square of land on the southwest corner of Yonge and modern College Streets, extending westward to Teraulay Street (as that part of Bay Street was called until 1923) and south to Hayter Street. He built Wickham Lodge on this square.

Wickham Lodge faced east to Yonge Street and stood about 450 feet west of the entrance gate. Much of the original pine forest was still standing on the Yonge Street side, and there were magnificent maples throughout the property. To the north were the fields of Elmsley Villa, home of the Judge's brother, John Simcoe Macaulay.

Wykeham Hall was originally Judge James Macauley's commodious Regency house, but between 1869 and 1914 it became the Bishop Strachan School and was much enlarged.

— Metropolitan Toronto Library Board

The house was only about a hundred feet south of College, but there could be no entrance there as College was a private road leading to King's College (now the University of Toronto). There were two College Avenues leading to King's College, which was most confusing. One was called "College Avenue west of Yonge," and ran to McCaul Street, the other (now University Avenue) "College Avenue north of Queen." Matters were further complicated by College Street, which ran west from McCaul Street. In an effort to clarify the situation the name of "College Avenue west from Yonge" was for a short time changed to Yonge Avenue. Of course, this was immediately confused with Yonge Street!

There were gates and caretakers' lodges at both Queen and Yonge entrances. College students had to be inside the gates by nine o'clock on winter evenings, when the gates were locked. If they were late they were "gated" (fined). In 1889 the gates were removed and both approaches became public streets.

Wickham was a two-storey brick house in the Regency manner, with a shallow roof, wide eaves, and three long windows in the front of the second storey. A deep bay on the south side carried up to the roof, with three windows in each storey. The large drawing room on the ground floor faced pleasant lawns and gardens on both east and south sides.

In 1849 Macaulay became Chief Justice of Common Pleas and ten years later he was knighted. In 1859 Sir James died. Curiously, soon after, Lady Macaulay changed the spelling of Wickham to "Wykeham."

In 1869 Bishop Strachan School, which had been occupying the Palace of the late Bishop, purchased Wykeham Lodge from the Macaulay family, and, after some changes, took possession in January 1870. The school was to occupy it for forty-five years. During this time it was always called Wykeham Hall.

In 1880 during a boom period in Toronto real estate, Bishop Strachan School sold a strip, 185 feet wide, bordering Yonge Street. The price of $11,000 was most satisfactory, and permitted much-needed enlargements to be made to the school.

Two wings were added to the west side of Wykeham Hall, similar to the original house, and a third storey was added above the entire building. A large square belvedere adorned the centre of the roof, with long windows on the four sides from which a splendid view in all directions could be enjoyed. The front entrance was now from the centre of the south side, and there were large balconies on the second and third floors above the main porch.

The large grounds provided such games as were considered suitable for young ladies. At first the only outdoor exercise the girls got was walking around a gravel oval at the east side and picking wild strawberries and violets, which abounded under the huge trees in early summer. Later they played "Bat and Ball," a lady-like imitation of baseball and "Prisoner's Base." There were croquet lawns and a cricket field. Later tennis courts, a bicycle track, and a nine-hole putting green were added. In winter there was a skating rink.

The drawing room of Wykeham Hall during Judge Macauley's occupancy. This large, pleasant room looked out over Yonge and College Streets and a vista of lawns and gardens. — Metropolitan Toronto Library Board

In 1888 a beautiful chapel was added in a wing to the rear of the original house. This wing extended almost to the wooden fence along College Street. About 1903 a new addition was added to the school, and a new two-manual organ installed in the chapel. The verandah on the east side of the original house was modernized, a balustrade added, and a small balcony built above the north end.

In 1914 the property was sold, although the school remained there until their new building on Lonsdale Road was ready. Wykeham Hall then housed the Central Military Convalescent Hospital, which became a neurological centre. After the War, the Hospital closed and the buildings became the College Street Armouries. In 1929 Wykeham Hall was vacant. It was then bought by the T. Eaton Company and demolished to make way for their College Street store, which opened in 1930.

A bronze plaque in the building commemorates Bishop Strachan School.

The Home Wood
1847-1964

Those who remember the original Wellesley Hospital will remember The Home Wood, the romantic Gothic Revival house designed by John G. Howard for George William Allan.

George, born in York in 1822, was the only son of the Honourable William Allan of the Family Compact. He was called to the Bar in 1846 and three months later married Louisa, daughter of Chief Justice (Sir) John B. Robinson. It was a double wedding (Louisa's sister Emily married John Lefroy) and a brilliant social occasion. Bishop Strachan officiated and all of Toronto's Establishment came to Beverley House for the reception.

George's father had bought Park Lot 5 and built his pillared Moss Park on the west side of Sherbourne Street, north of Queen Street. He gave George the north half of the Moss Park lot, fifty acres between Carleton Street (as then spelled) and Bloor Street, and west from Sherbourne to Jarvis Street. The land was covered with forest and the young couple called it and their villa "The Home Wood." Moss Park and Home Wood were names of Allan family farms in Scotland.

The Home Wood was built on the north side of modern Wellesley Street, a little west of today's Sherbourne Street, then called Allan's Lane. The approach was from a gatehouse lodge near the northwest corner of Carleton Street. The long driveway wound through pine woods, made a circle in front of the house, and continued northeast to the brick stables and coach house.

A painting of The Home Wood, George Allan's haunting Gothic Revival house, by Paul Kane. The Allans did not like the painting because it showed the tree stumps still in the foreground.

— J. Russell Harper

The house, three storeys high, faced south and was of rosy red brick with stone trim. The entrance was in the middle, with double doors in a Gothic stone arch and a high, pointed fanlight. A square stone above the door bore the date 1848 and the Allan coat-of-arms. On each side was a wide bay with long, triple Gothic windows set in carved stone, with a balcony above. One entered the wide front hall through a triple mahogany archway, and the imposing staircase had carved mahogany balusters and a magnificent stained-glass window at the landing. All hall doors were set in Gothic arches of carved wood.

George Allan was one of the first to recognize the genius of Paul Kane, the Irish painter who travelled to the Pacific sketching Indian life. Allan became Kane's friend and patron, and in 1848 Allan com-

The conservatory or Palm Room of Homewood was added on by Frederic Nicholls when he bought the house in 1900, and was typical of the time.

— Mrs. C. Gardner

missioned him to paint The Home Wood. There was a sharp difference of opinion when Kane depicted the raw stumps still in the foreground, but it is this realism that makes Kane's paintings valuable today.

The Allans did not enjoy The Home Wood for long. The house was isolated, Louisa was delicate, and they travelled extensively. While touring Europe in 1852, the twenty-six-year-old Louisa died of tuberculosis in Rome. There were no children.

When his father died the next year, George inherited Moss Park. He rented The Home Wood and moved back to his old home. He bought Kane's series of western paintings and Indian artifacts for $20,000 and the superb collection hung at Moss Park until his death in 1901, when Sir Edmund Osler bought it and later presented it to the Royal Ontario Museum.

George Allan was Mayor of Toronto, a Legislative Councillor, Chief Commissioner of the Canada Company, Speaker of the Senate, and Chancellor of Trinity University. He was one of Toronto's most prominent citizens.

The Reverend Thomas Schreiber rented The Home Wood. He was

Homewood was the first house in Toronto with electricity, and the ornate gasoliers, such as the one above in the drawing room, were wired from a private power plant.
— Mrs. C. Gardner

an English clergyman with fifteen lively children and private means (fortunately). The Home Wood became the scene of many gay parties and picnics which often were attended by the landlord. For Allan it was a pleasant half-mile ride from Moss Park to his former home.

Schreiber planted a large orchard and improved the formal flower gardens, gradually replacing the bush. Greenhouses, smooth lawns, and summer houses filled the "pleasure grounds."

After his wife died in 1857, Schreiber returned to England. Soon after George Allan went to London and married Adelaide Schreiber, the Reverend Thomas Schreiber's daughter. They returned to Toronto, lived at Moss Park, and had seven children.

"George Allan was president of everything cultural and horticultural that happened in Toronto — the Historical Society, Ontario Society of Artists, Conservatory of Music, Horticultural Society, and the Royal Canadian Institute," wrote a reporter of the time. He gave five acres of land between Gerrard and Carlton Streets to the Toronto Horticultural Society, and in 1860 the grounds were opened by the Prince of Wales. The Society gave the enlarged grounds, with their

George W. Allan (1822-1901) was one of Toronto's most prominent citizens. Besides his many civic and political posts, he was "president of everything cultural and horticultural in Toronto."

— Ontario Archives

Palm House, to the city in 1888, and in 1901 the park was named Allan Gardens.

Allan subdivided the bush north of The Home Wood to Bloor Street and opened new streets, Huntley on the west and Selby, Linden, and Isabella running east and west. The area soon built up. The Home Wood, shorn of its Jarvis and Bloor Street frontage still extended south to Carlton and east to Sherbourne, with Isabella as its northern boundary.

Benjamin Homer Dixon, Canadian Consul General of the Netherlands, leased the property for several years. In 1863 he bought it for £5,000. His wife Kate was a daughter of Chief Justice Sir James Macaulay of Wykeham Hall; thus the wives of the first two owners of The Home Wood were daughters of the Chief Justice of the day.

In 1865, Homewood, as henceforth spelled, was further subdivided, as land north of Gloucester Street and along Sherbourne Street was sold, leaving the estate 330 feet wide, with Wellesley Place as its western boundary.

Mrs. Dixon died in 1865 and the following year Dixon married Frances Heward, who died in 1889. The widower then married youthful Emilia Caston in 1891. Dixon was a Director of the Toronto General Trust Company and of the Evangelical Publishing Company and wrote several religious works.

From 1897 to 1900 Homewood stood vacant. Then it was bought by Frederic Nicholls, an Englishman who came to Ottawa in 1874, and, in a romantic elopement, married sixteen-year-old Florence Graburn who was at school in a Quebec convent. They moved to Toronto where Frederic became interested in electricity and in 1888 formed a syndicate for electrical development. The Toronto Construction and Electrical Supply Company was formed with Nicholls at its head. The company laid the first underground wires in Canada amid much derision. The (American) Edison General Electric Company was a strong rival for the Canadian market, but Nicholls bought the Edison Company in Peterborough and the merger grew into the Canadian General Electric Company with Nicholls as president. After other power and railway company mergers, he became a powerful Canadian industrialist.

When he bought Homewood, Nicholls installed electricity in the house from a private power plant, wiring the ornate gasoliers. It was the first house in Toronto with electricity.

Nicholls was fond of flowers, always wearing an orchid from his own greenhouses in his buttonhole. He landscaped the grounds, adding a gazebo near the tennis courts. He built a new wing north of the conservatory (or Palm Room) and opening from it. The addition, with walnut woodwork, contained a smoking room and a billiard room, both with cove ceilings, Doric columns, and brick fireplaces. The billiard room also served as a gallery for his fine collection of Turners, Gainsboroughs, and many other paintings.

Nicholls was vice-consul for Argentina and Liberia, a director of Bishop Ridley College, and a Canadian senator. The Nicholls entertained constantly. Mrs. Nicholls was a charming hostess and, having seven children, the house was full of life. All were keen riders of the fine horses in the stables.

In 1909 Mrs. Nicholls died and Homewood was sold soon after. Dr. Herbert Bruce, a brilliant, successful surgeon bought Homewood and its remaining four and a half acres for $65,000 for a private hospital. He was helped financially by Sir William Mulock and Sir Edmund Osler, who became trustees of the hospital — which was named "Wellesley." Sturdy old Homewood was remodelled for a new career. Partitions converted spacious rooms into smaller ones, fire escapes were added, and most of the fireplaces were bricked up. The Palm Room became the Men's Ward with curtained cubicles, and a large verandah with balcony was built on the east side. Dr. Bruce received permission from the Duke of Wellington, whose family name was Wellesley, to use his crest and motto, "Jamais sans Esperance," for the hospital, and it was put on the blue and white china specially made in Limoges.

The new hospital was formally opened in 1911 by Sir Wilfrid Laurier.

In 1916 Wellesley became a public hospital, and Dr. Bruce went on to new honours. In 1932 he became Lieutenant Governor of Ontario, the last to live in Government House at Chorley Park.

Wellesley Hospital, with Homewood as its nucleus, was enlarged

Mrs. Frederic Nicholls and a friend in front of Homewood in 1905.

— Mrs. C. Gardner

and modernized over the years until it outgrew its usefulness. In 1964 patients were moved to temporary quarters in the nurses' residence, and Homewood was demolished.

When Mrs. Bruce furnished a "quiet room" in the new hospital in memory of Dr. Bruce, she donated some of the lovely windows from the Palm Room, and a set of the china with the Wellesley crest and the fine English silver, used by early patients, may still be seen in a case in the lounge of the new nurses' residence. The low brick wall, with stone coping and iron cresting, still extends along Wellesley Crescent, but the tall wrought-iron gates, with the name "Home Wood" above them, were taken by the wreckers. Painted a shocking orange, they now adorn the entrance to the wreckers' headquarters.

Oakham House
1848-

It is interesting to see what style an architect will adopt when he designs his own house. In old Toronto there were a number of houses built by architects for themselves. John G. Howard built Colborne Lodge in what is now High Park, Frederick Cumberland built Pendarvis on St. George Street, and William Thomas built Oakham House as his home and office. Oakham House's style has variously been described as Tudor Gothic, Victorian Gothic, Picturesque Gothic, Domestic Gothic, Gothic Revival, Decorated Gothic, and Fake Gothic, so we may safely conclude that Oakham House is indeed Gothic.

Oakham House still stands on the southwest corner of Gould and Church Streets. It has been called the best example of domestic Gothic in Toronto, but today its exterior is shorn of some of its most interesting details and its interior completely shorn of all interesting details.

William Thomas was born in 1800 in Stroud, Gloucestershire, England, the son of an innkeeper. When he was twelve years old he was apprenticed to a master carpenter for seven years. At that time master carpenters were architects, builders, contractors, and joiners, and were frequently skilled carvers in wood and stone.

Thomas was a tall, handsome man with a charming smile and curly hair and beard. He lived for some years in Leamington, Warwickshire, where he designed Lansdowne Crescent and Circus, at least one church, and a number of houses. Leamington is about forty miles from

Oakham House in 1876. It is probably the best example of domestic Gothic architecture in Toronto, although today it is shorn of some of its most interesting details. — *Illustrated Toronto Past and Present*, 1876

Oakham in Rutland County, where William had relatives. He would have been familiar with Oakham Castle there, which may have influenced his choice of a name for his Toronto house.

In 1843 William came to Canada with his wife, Martha Tutin, five sons, and five daughters. He settled in Toronto, but for some years maintained an office in Hamilton as well. He designed public buildings in Toronto, London, Cobourg, and Hamilton. Like other architects of the day, he was also a surveyor and engineer, and when John G. Howard was away in England in 1853, it was William Thomas who took his place as City Engineer.

His work had an impressive dignity, and, although Thomas spent only seventeen years in Canada, his influence on the architecture of the day was strong. He also trained a number of young architects, exerting a good influence on the profession. Two of his sons became architects.

Thomas's earliest work in Toronto is still standing. The building was designed for the Commercial Bank at 15 Wellington Street West

William Thomas designed many public buildings, but his best known works are the St. Lawrence Hall and the Don Jail. He loved to use carved stone heads to embellish his buildings, and Oakham House's front façade is decorated with carved heads of his wife and himself.

— Metropolitan Toronto Library Board

118   *Toronto: 100 Years of Grandeur*

and is now used as offices. Carefully preserved, this handsome building with its elegant iron balconies is a fine example of Thomas's classical style. But his best known work is St. Lawrence Hall on King Street East, for many years Toronto's social and entertainment centre. With its impressive façade, its beautiful Great Hall, and its carved embellishments, St. Lawrence Hall is proof of Thomas's mastery of the classic Revival style.

Thomas had a penchant for sculptured stone heads on his buildings. (The head on the right side of the Palace door is said to represent Bishop Power.) When he designed the Don Jail he set a large bearded head on the keystone above the front door. He set heads of river gods, St. Lawrence in the centre, above the arches of St. Lawrence Hall, with carved heads of Jupiter, Apollo, Music, and Mirth elsewhere on the building. Of course he had no monopoly on the use of carved heads. Delightful heads of various sizes, expressions, and curly beards gaze down from many nineteenth century buildings. They are to be seen in fascinating detail on theatres, colleges, and firehalls. Banks seemed especially fond of heads as keystones in arches above entrances. The architect Lennox and a number of Toronto dignitaries can be recognized in the stone heads on the Old City Hall. William Thomas, however, was unique in that he used carved heads on the façade of his own residence.

The Crown land which Thomas bought for $500 was on the fringe of the built-up part of the city. The lot ran westward from Church Street (which ended at Carlton Street) to a lane halfway to Bond Street. In 1848 there were no buildings visible to the north, and there were only stumps, weeds, and swamp across Gould Street where the Normal School would be built four years later.

Oakham House was built of the usual greyish Toronto brick. It occupied the north half of the lot, while the south half was garden. The house was well built on a stone foundation and both outer walls and inner partitions were three bricks thick.

At the curb facing each other were two large iron dogs with iron rings in their mouths for hitching horses. They were painted red to represent Chesapeake Bay Retrievers. Later, when horse traffic decreased and the street was widened, the life-size dogs were removed

Oakham House in 1949. Note the beasts on the gables and the dogs by the front door.

— Panda Associates

from the curb and mounted at the front entrance, one on each side of the steps.

Originally the narrow end of the house with its twin gables facing Church Street was the front. On each side of the front door is a crowned head carved in stone, male on the left and female on the right. Both ground floor windows have charming sculptured heads; those on the south window almost certainly represent Thomas and his wife.

Beautifully carved heads with garlands on their brows are at the base of the four slender pinnacles. This makes a total of ten heads on the façade of Oakham House, all different and all delightful! It is possible that Thomas carved the Gothic corbelled heads himself.

Below the centre window above the door is a square with an ornate T with a small shield on each side, with heraldic devices. The carved stone sign "Oakham House," which was once above the front door, and the two iron dogs, which formerly guarded the front steps, have

Details of the front doorway of Oakham House. Carved in stone, the crowned head on the left is male, the right female.

— Toronto Historical Board

been removed. There is some mystery concerning the fate of the carved stone animals which originally stared over Church Street from the highest peak of the gables. A lordly lion sat on the south gable, but it was not a unicorn, as might have been expected, which sat on the north gable. It was some prehistoric creature resembling a dinosaur, with reptilian head and long, heavy tail, which Thomas's whim set high above Oakham House. These delightful beasts were there until 1952, when they were removed because it was said they were crumbling dangerously. Where are they now?

The front hall had coloured murals depicting rural scenes. The roof was of slate, and the eavestroughs and pinnacle ornaments were of heavy copper which soon turned an attractive shade of green. The grounds, although small, were attractive, with an arbour in the centre, a number of statues, and a tall flagpole.

In 1854 William Thomas designed the monument to General Sir Isaac Brock, high on Queenston Heights. It replaced the one which some crazed Americans had blown up, and Brock's body was interred again. Surely the gallant Brock is unique in having three public funerals, the last one forty-two years after the first!

Thomas died in 1860. Shortly before his death he sold Oakham House for $2,000 to John McGee, iron founder, stove manufacturer, and relative of D'Arcy McGee. The house remained in the McGee family until 1898, when the City bought it for $8,000, and for the next sixty years Oakham House was the Working Boys' Home.

The large rooms were cut into cubicles, the high plaster ceilings were covered with galvanized tin to lower their height for easier heating, and the murals were covered by a coat of calcimine.

About fifty teen-age problem boys received room and board and some counselling, for which they were expected to pay a modest sum. A small staff lived in the house, and there were many dedicated Toronto ladies who contributed their services. The boys themselves did much of the cleaning.

Sometime in the 1940s the calcimine was washed from the walls, and the old murals came to light again. The red paint on the iron dogs got shabby and they were given a coat of black paint, which changed them to Labrador Retrievers.

In October 1958 the Ontario Government bought Oakham House for the Ryerson Polytechnical Institute.

By various ingenious methods Ryerson students amassed a fund of $100,000 to completely transform old Oakham House for their use as a Student Union Building. It took two years to fumigate, clean up, and restore the interior.

In November 1960 the Student Union Building was renamed "Kerr Hall" in honour of Principal H.H. Kerr and opened. The old frescoes in the drawing room are now covered by imitation mahogany panels, and Swedish modern furniture fills the rooms which once saw the opulence of Victorian furnishings. Kerr Hall is modern and functional, but bears no trace of picturesque Oakham House.

Northfield
1855-

Today Northfield is the Canadian Broadcasting Corporation's Toronto headquarters, but it has led a number of lives since Oliver Mowat, a brilliant lawyer from Kingston, built it. In 1846 Oliver married Jane Ewart, the daughter of a contractor who built many public buildings in Toronto and invested the profits in land. Ewart owned a large block of land on the west side of Jarvis Street north of Carlton Street, extending back to Mutual Street. In 1855 he gave Jane and Oliver a lot 260 feet wide and 141 feet deep. They immediately built a house on it, which they called "Northfield," because only open fields could be seen to the north. At that time Jarvis Street was a sandy road with a small creek running down its west side.

Northfield is a fine example of classic symmetry. Built of yellowish brick (now painted grey), the main part is a large square block with wide eaves handsomely bracketed and four tall, double chimneys linked at the top. There is a narrower, lower wing in the rear. A wide verandah originally extended along the south side of the house, and there was a brick stable and coach house in the rear. Lawns and flower beds filled the space between house and picket fence at the street.

The main block contained two storeys and a shallow attic. Double front doors of solid oak with a rectangular light above and on each side opened to a vestibule. Another pair of doors led to the wide centre hall with its fine ceiling plasterwork. All the rooms were spacious, with lofty ceilings, and they stayed cool even on the hottest days.

A wide arch in the hall leads to the graceful curving staircase, the slender newel post enclosed in a small cage — a charming classical detail. The window at the landing, now clear, was once of coloured glass, splashing the hall with bright light from the afternoon sun. A high, rounded niche to the right of the window, now plastered over, may have once held a decorative lamp to light the stairs.

The year 1861 was a time of depression in Upper Canada, and many people had to sell their property and carriages, Oliver Mowat among them. He sold his fine house and moved to smaller quarters. (He later became a Father of Confederation and was Premier of Ontario for a record twenty-four years. In 1892 he became Sir Oliver.)

Edward Rutherford bought Northfield, then known as 350 Jarvis Street, for £4,550. On the same day he bought from the Ewart estate a strip of land fifty feet wide across the rear. There was still only vacant ground northward to one block north of Wellesley Street.

Rutherford, born in Ireland, was Vice-President of the Bank of Upper Canada, a director of the Canada Permanent Building Society, and later President of the Consumers' Gas Company. During the long period when the Rutherfords occupied Northfield, Jarvis Street was at the height of its glory. The mansions of the prosperous and the power-ful stood in large grounds behind ornate iron fences. The wide, tree-lined avenue with its grassy boulevards was a desirable place to live.

Rutherford planted apple and pear orchards south of the house — the fruit proving an irresistible temptation to the girls at Havergal, the private school next door. Tennis courts were built, and lilac bushes hid the front fence. A new entrance to the stables was made from Mutual Street in the rear, and a carriageway wound to a circle in front of the house.

The Rutherfords had two sons and six daughters. Frequent visits were exchanged with the Goldwin Smiths of The Grange and the Jarvis, Mason, and Blake families of Jarvis Street.

Rutherford died in 1884, his widow in 1913. Northfield was bought by Havergal Ladies' College, which occupied buildings next door and across the road. The school's small sandy yard was impossible for games, and although they had already bought a piece of land from

Today Northfield on Jarvis Street north of Carlton is the headquarters of the Canadian Broadcasting Corporation, but it has led a chequered life since Oliver Mowat, a brilliant lawyer from Kingston, built it in 1855. He called it "Northfield" because only open fields could be seen to the north.

— Canadian Broadcasting Corporation

Mrs. Rutherford in 1896, the young ladies still lacked proper grounds for their decorous exercises. For years both staff and girls had been eyeing Northfield's pleasant gardens.

Miss Wood, later the headmistress, moved with some teachers and senior girls into Northfield. The girls, daughters of well-to-do families, studied domestic science here. They paid sizable fees to cook,

Between 1913 and 1935 Northfield was part of Havergal Ladies College and its lawns became the girls' playgrounds.

— Havergal College

sweep, wash windows, and make simple repairs. One gathers they hugely enjoyed themselves. A previous group of Old Girls had formed the Coverly Club, suggested by a country dance they liked and soon Northfield became Coverly House.

Windows were opened in the roof providing bedrooms in the attic. Three dormer windows each on east, north, and south sides, and two in the rear give the house its unusual pierced cornice.

Havergal replaced the lilac hedge with a forbidding board fence ten feet high, topped by three strands of barbed wire. For a generation this handsome house was hidden from passersby. Tennis and basketball courts, which became skating rinks in winter, covered lawns and gardens.

In the 1930s Havergal College was bursting its seams again. The school bought twenty-seven acres at Avenue Road and Lawrence Avenue. The scattered buildings of the school were sold, and, interestingly, the Board estimated the Jarvis Street buildings to be worth $350,000! And this was 1935, at the height of the Depression.

Old Northfield stood empty until the Second World War, when the Canadian Government bought it for a training depot for the Canadian Women's Air Force. To the annoyance of the school, it became known as the "Havergal Manning Pool for Women," and was listed as such in the City Directory.

The Air Force modernized the old house. They installed steam heating, modernized the basement, put up partitions, and paved the playgrounds. The sophisticated young women in uniform who succeeded the schoolgirls soon transformed the atmosphere of Coverly House!

After the war the Canadian Broadcasting Corporation took over. It cleaned up all signs of military occupation and, in 1946, moved in. The house, first Northfield then Coverly became "The Annex," but was called "The Kremlin" by the staff, since high level decisions were made there.

Today, the old red brick Havergal is the radio division, and an ugly, yellow brick building in the rear is the television division. A tall iron tower, similar to the windmills which once marked artesian wells and also resembling Mr. Eiffel's Paris creation, sprang up in 1961.

Northfield houses the executive offices of the Toronto branch of the Canadian Broadcasting Corporation. The former dining room, where heavy Victorian dinners were once consumed, is the board room.

The vestibule doors are gone. A single, modern front door replaces the double doors, and tiles replace the hall carpet. But the house has been handsomely restored, with a mimimum of alterations.

Lucky Northfield! Many Jarvis Street mansions have been demolished; Northfield has not only survived but has adapted to our day and age.

Sherborne Villa
1857-1964

Everyone laughed when Thomas Gibbs Ridout built his house in the midst of an unbroken forest, and they ridiculed the house, calling it the "Acre House" because of its great size. Thomas spent a fortune on his house but never lived in it.

In 1818 Thomas's half-brother Samuel bought Park Lot 4 from the White estate for $2,400. The property, extending from modern Queen Street to Bloor Street, contained one hundred acres and had been a Crown grant to the Attorney General John White who was killed in a duel by Major John Small of Berkeley House. Some years later Samuel sold the west half of the lot to Thomas.

Thomas was born in 1792, and for forty years he was cashier (managing director) of the Bank of Upper Canada.

In 1844 Thomas wrote to the Toronto City Council saying he had laid out a public road along his western boundary and he wished it to be named Sherborne Street, after the county town in Dorsetshire, England — his father's birthplace.

Thomas then sold much of the land along Sherborne Street but retained a large lot between Carlton and Howard Streets. In 1857 he laid the foundations of the mansion he called Sherborne Villa. There was no u in the spelling then; it crept in later.

Sherborne Villa was designed by Frederick Cumberland, architect of University College, whose wife was Ridout's wife's sister. The house resembled Cumberland's own home, Pendarvis, and The Hall which he designed for Sir Casimir Gzowski.

Sherborne Villa was at the height of its glory in 1912 when it was owned by George A. Cox, a financier, who changed the arrangement of the rooms to better accommodate his large scale entertainments.

— *Toronto Canada's Queen City*, 1912

Sherborne Villa did not belong to any particular style of architecture, but it had many features of the Italianate villa style, particularly the irregular outline and the wide, bracketed eaves. Unfortunately, while he was building his house, the Bank of Upper Canada where Ridout lived and worked, was near collapse. Ridout was nearly ruined. He had to sell Sherborne Villa and give up his horses and carriage and in 1861 he died, leaving his splendid villa still empty and not quite finished.

The first occupant was Secker Brough, an Irish barrister. He lived at Sherborne for about three years until he was appointed a judge and moved to Goderich.

In 1867 Henry S. Howland who had milling and railroad interests bought the house. His brother was Sir William P. Howland who became Lieutenant Governor of Ontario in that Confederation year. The Henry Howland family lived in Sherborne for twenty years, and the house, which for so long had been the only one on the east side between

Gerrard and Bloor Streets, eventually became 409 Sherborne Street.

In 1888 the big white brick house with its extensive grounds was bought by Senator George A. Cox, a financier. He lived there until he died in 1914. By this time the street was fringed by opulent mansions and had become a good address.

During the Cox years it was the scene of many parties, and the arrangement of the rooms changed. The eastern end of the verandah on the south was closed in to form a large conservatory. A handsome glass and wrought-iron canopy, supported on slender iron pillars, was added to the front entrance. This graceful canopy extended from the roof of the porch and shielded family and guests from the elements.

Sherborne Villa stood about ninety feet back from the street on a lot two hundred feet wide which extended back to Bleecker Street. A wrought-iron fence, set above a low wall of red sandstone, with pillars at intervals, ran across the front of the property.

A circular driveway with wrought-iron gates led to the open porch. The porch had Corinthian columns and a balustraded balcony above. The main floor windows were rectangular, but those on the second floor, single, double, and triple in their grouping, were Italianate in style. The grounds were landscaped with ornamental trees and shrubs. Stables and a carriage house were in the northeast corner.

The double front doors were made of heavy mahogany; the upper part of Belgian crystal, set in lead in a scrolled design. A vestibule opened into a huge hall with a rich wood wainscot, the walls above being covered by a silk brocade woven in England — the soft moss green colour of the pattern resembled a fleur-de-lis. All ceilings were fifteen feet high.

An archway to the right of the front entrance led to the drawing room, whose Adam ceiling was of moulded white plaster in a lovely design. The drawing room opened through a square archway, with Corinthian columns, to the music room. The walls of both rooms were covered by apple green watered silk, the pattern the same as that of the hall and stairway, but lighter. Identical Adams fireplaces in the drawing room and music room were of a rosy veined marble.

The dining room, behind the music room, had French doors to the sunroom, as did the music room. The walls of the dining room were of

The hallway and library of Sherborne Villa in 1949, when it had become Fudger House, a home for The Robert Simpson Company's women employees. Note the beautiful carved wainscot.

— Robert Simpson Company Archives

Italian tooled leather in a maroon colour above oak wainscotting. The ceiling, with a dropped cornice, had a design of moulded leaves and flowers in a curved border. The oak mantel had an Italian plaque above it, similar to cloissonée.

To the left of the front door was a reception room with a fireplace on the north wall. A rounded archway led to a library of impressive proportions, with bookcases of rich cherry wood. At the end of the fireplace on the east wall were concealed doors to two washrooms, which could also be entered from doors in the hall under the stairs. French windows in both the reception room and library opened to the garden.

The grand staircase turned at a wide landing, but instead of the usual window on the landing, the stairway was lighted by a coloured glass skylight.

In 1916 beautiful Sherborne Villa was sold to H.H. Fudger, President of the Robert Simpson Company, who set up a foundation to provide a home for out-of-town women employees. An addition was built in the rear, which contained one hundred and fifty bedrooms, a large dining room, kitchen, and laundry. A delightful roof garden was a favourite feature, and the tennis courts on the south side of the house were enlarged. Much of Senator Cox's walnut furniture stayed in the house.

The new home for Simpson girls, renamed Fudger House, opened in 1917. For nearly fifty years thousands of lonely girls found an inexpensive, comfortable home amid the surroundings of an earlier era. Hundreds of weddings were held here. However, as time went on, there was not such a demand for an employees' home and it was sold to the City of Toronto for $400,000 who handed it over to the Toronto General Hospital.

In April 1964 the wreckers descended on Sherborne Villa. Today a modern, high-rise home for the aged sits on the site.

The wrought-iron canopy went to a group who planned to use it above a drive-through in Clarence Square where rowhouses were being restored, but the plan had to be abandoned. For two years the canopy reposed on the new owner's lawn in York Mills, to the great astonishment of passersby. In 1970 it was installed at the entrance to an old house on the south side of Elm Avenue.

Culloden
1858-

The old house is still there — on the east side of Sherbourne Street south of Gerrard Street. Today it is the Training and Development Centre of the Ontario Provincial Police, but for many years it was John Ross Robertson's handsome, comfortable home.

The first occupant, in 1858, was a Dr. James Forneri, an Italian professor with a reputation of having survived incredible adventures in France, Russia, Spain, and Ireland. At this time there was only one house on Sherbourne Street between 151 and Bloor Street. Fields and forests stretched northward.

In 1872 Captain John Douglas, Customs Collector, bought the house. Nine years later he sold it to John Ross Robertson. By that time it had become number 257.

John R. Robertson was born in Toronto in 1841. He was the son of John Robertson, a wholesale dry goods merchant, who had been born in Scotland near the moor of Culloden — the spot where Stuart hopes were crushed in 1746.

John was educated at Upper Canada College where he founded the *College Times* in 1857. He set type on a hand machine, sold subscriptions, and was editor, writer, and publisher. His schoolmates so enjoyed his bloodcurdling serials that when publication suddenly ceased, they were enraged at not knowing how the hero had escaped. John did not have enough money to pay them back for their subscriptions, so they beat him thoroughly. This painful experience was a useful lesson to the budding editor. It is interesting to note that the school paper, after various changes, is still the *College Times*.

John went on to work on several Toronto newspapers. In 1871 he married Maria Gilbee. They moved to London, England, where John was correspondent for the Toronto *Globe* and their son, John Sinclair, was born there. Returning to Toronto he became manager of *The Nation*, edited by Goldwin Smith. Smith encouraged him to found an independent paper and even loaned him $10,000. In 1876 Robertson launched *The Evening Telegram*, "with no patron but the public," a four-page journal selling at two cents a copy. Soon it was lowered to one cent, and circulation skyrocketed.

In 1880 John and Maria's only daughter, Helen Goldwin, was born, but Goldie, as they called her, died of scarlet fever less than a year later.

In 1881 Robertson bought the Sherbourne Street house and called it "Culloden." Their second son, Irving Earle, was born there the following year.

Culloden was a centre hall house with a deep bay on the north side and with a tall gable above it. A wide verandah extended across the front at the right of the entrance and along the south side. Many features of the Italianate style — narrow roundheaded windows, deep-bracketed cornice, and slender verandah columns — characterize the house.

In the rear was the brick coach house with a turret on the slate roof and groom's quarters in the loft. A stable held fine coach horses which won many ribbons at annual shows.

Robertson had the drawing room ceiling painted in a floral pattern in delicate tints; the tooled leather wainscot in the hall was green and amber. This four-foot wainscot in upper and lower halls and dining room is still there.

The dining room had a square bay on the south side with narrow windows and a fireplace on the hall side. The high wooden mantel had a large carved mirror above it. A cheery sunroom off the east end of the room was the morning room. John closed in the porch over the front door and it became Maria's sewing room, known as "the lookout."

Culloden, the comfortable Victorian home of John Robertson, founder of *The Evening Telegram*. Note the Boy with the Boot fountain behind the picket fence.

— Metropolitan Toronto Library Board

A black lead fountain, appropriate for a newspaper publisher, sat on the front lawn. In the form of a ragged newsboy holding a leaking boot and enjoying the water streaming from the heel, it became a neighbourhood landmark.

In 1886 Maria died. Two years later John married Jessie Holland, "the girl next door."

Because of what had happened to Goldie, John became dedicated to bettering medical care for suffering children, and it was he who was the guiding spirit behind the Lakeside Home for Little Children on Toronto Island, where sick children could grow strong in the fresh air.

Toronto did have the small Hospital for Sick Children founded in 1875 by a group of benevolent women headed by Mrs. Samuel

McMaster, but it lacked funds and facilities. During his annual holidays John studied hospitals. He found his ideal in Glasgow. He asked its architect to draft plans for a similar building in Toronto, and, on his return, gave the plans to architects Darling and Curry.

John now started a campaign for a new, well-equipped hospital. He himself donated large sums to make it possible, and his constant publicity in *The Evening Telegram* gained the support of influential citizens. On June 10, 1889, his son Irving turned the first sod for the new Hospital for Sick Children on the south side of College Street east of Elizabeth Street.

In 1891 Robertson became first Chairman of the Board of Trustees, a position he held until his death. The same year, in memory of Goldie and his first wife, he installed a large stained-glass window in the hospital entrance. Years later this window, depicting Christ healing a little girl seated on her mother's lap, was installed in the new building on University Avenue.

At his own expense he built a milk-pasteurizing plant at the hospital. At this time the paper was making large profits, which then of course were not drained away by high taxes. John put his fortune to good use. He constantly improved the hospital and he visited it every morning. Year after year he delighted the small patients by acting as Santa Claus, and sometimes nurses dressed as reindeer drew Santa's sleigh through the wards.

He used his influence to create the policy that no child in need of medical care would ever be refused because of race, creed, or poverty. His paper publicized the hospital's work and made constant appeals for it. With help from other benefactors, he built a five-storey residence for student nurses as a memorial to Maria.

The Boy with Boot fountain in front of Culloden became a great magnet for neighbourhood children — they tried to pull the boot out of his hand. Finally, one hot day the second Mrs. Robertson was horrified to find a group of naked urchins splashing in the basin at the foot of the fountain! The boy and his leaky boot were banished to the back, but they were unknowingly set over an abandoned well and soon collapsed into a deep hole. Twelve wagonloads of ashes were needed to fill the hole and provide a solid base for the fountain!

One of John's hobbies was collecting maps and pictures of early Canada, particularly Toronto. He travelled widely in search of material and he employed agents in both Britain and Canada in the constant quest. The halls and rooms of Culloden were hung with photographs, engravings, watercolours, and oil paintings. His library, a large room on the south side of the second floor at the front, was filled with cabinets of manuscripts, pamphlets, scrapbooks, and pictures of early Toronto. His enormous carved desk stood in the square bay on the south side in the light of four tall windows. A rich Oriental rug covered the floor, and a square, revolving bookstand, made from the countertop in the Treasurer's office in the first City Hall on Front Street, was filled with reference works. It was in this library that he dictated his famous *Landmarks of Toronto*. Published first in *The Evening Telegram*, *Landmarks* appeared in six volumes from 1894 to 1914. John commissioned artists such as Owen Staples to illustrate the work.

John was also a dedicated Freemason. In 1890 he became Grand Master of the Grand Lodge of Canada. When Sir John A. Macdonald died in 1891 Robertson succeeded him as Grand Representative of the Grand Lodge of England in Canada, and his monumental illustrated *History of Freemasonry in Canada* was written in the library at Culloden.

From 1896 to 1900 he sat in the House of Commons as an independent Conservative for East Toronto.

About 1912 Robertson bought the property north of Culloden and gave the use of the house to the graduate nurses of Toronto for a central registry and clubhouse. He then built a new wing on the north side of Culloden, duplicating the deep bay containing the original drawing room. A square arch with Corinthian columns joined the two sections. Most drawing rooms of the day were double, the two rooms usually end to end, but at Culloden the rooms were side by side.

John visited the Simcoe home in Devonshire and returned with the diary kept by Mrs. Simcoe during her years in Upper Canada when Colonel Simcoe was the first governor. In 1912 he edited and published this valuable diary, with notes and reproductions of Mrs. Simcoe's sketches.

He was also president of the Canadian Associated Press and in 1914 was elected a fellow of the Royal Society of Canada. In 1917 he was offered a knighthood and a senatorship, but he declined both honours — on the same day.

Robertson always said, "Don't let *The Telegram* miss an edition when I go", and when he died on May 30, 1918, the paper appeared as usual. His son, John Sinclair, always known as Culley, perhaps for Culloden, was a *Telegram* reporter for Police Court News, but poked so much fun at magistrates and police that he was transferred to Sports. Culley died three weeks after his father.

John's will provided an annual payment of $10,000.00 to the Hospital for Sick Children, and at the death of widow and sons, the bulk of the estate was to go to the hospital. Culloden's taxes and insurance would be paid by the estate. The priceless collection of historical papers and pictures and two of Simcoe's swords went to the Toronto Public Library.

In 1920 Mrs. Robertson (Jessie) married Irving Cameron, Chief Surgeon at the Toronto General Hospital. He moved into Culloden where he died in 1933. Mrs. Cameron remained there until her death in 1947. George McCullagh, publisher of *The Globe and Mail* paid $3,610,000.00 for *The Evening Telegram*. On his death in 1952 the paper was bought by John Bassett and associates.

Irving Robertson died in 1932, and after Jessie Cameron's death Irving's widow inherited Culloden. She bought Ainslie Hill farm near Sutton, Ontario and moved the furniture and Newsboy fountain from Culloden to Ainslie Hill.

The Ontario Government bought Culloden and set up an Immigration Centre managed by the Salvation Army, using the old Nurses' Registry next door also. The yellow brick of both houses was painted grey, the woodwork black.

In 1951 the Ontario Provincial Police took over the two houses. Culloden became a college with forty students in residence. Neat cots fill the library, the lawn is paved for a parade ground and Culloden is spick and span.

The Hall
1858-1904

The Hall was the home of the most romantic figure in nineteenth century Toronto.

Casimir Stanislaus Gzowski, a Polish nobleman, was an engineer, soldier, lawyer, contractor, financier, and aide-de-camp to Queen Victoria. He was born in St. Petersburg in 1813, the son of Count Stanislaus Gzowski, an officer in the Imperial Russian Guard. Casimir joined the Russian army and trained as an engineer, but in 1830 he helped Polish patriots in the expulsion of Czar Nicholas's brother Constantine from Warsaw. Casimir was wounded, captured, and condemned to death. At the last minute, because of his father's influence, the sentence was changed to exile.

Many adventures later he arrived in the United States. He was twenty-one years old, six feet four inches tall, and strikingly handsome, with fair hair and blue eyes. He spoke Polish, Russian, French, German, and Italian, but not enough English to practise as an engineer. To make ends meet he gave violin and language lessons, taught fencing, and articled in a law firm. Four years later Casimir took the oath of allegiance and was admitted to the Bar. The next year he married seventeen-year-old Maria Beebe, a pupil in the private school where he taught.

Gzowski became one of the engineers to build the New York and Erie Railway and he was sent to Canada, where he met Lord Sydenham, the Governor General. Sydenham had been to Russia on business for his father's trading company and had been entertained by Count Gzowski. He gave Casimir a post on the engineering staff of the Canadian Public Works Department. In 1846 Casimir became a British subject.

For the next seven years he dabbled in many things. He then founded a contracting company in Toronto with businessmen Galt and Macpherson. Together they built the Grand Trunk Railway from Toronto to Sarnia, and, as president of the Toronto Rolling Mills, Casimir amassed a large fortune.

In the mid 1850s he bought seven acres of land on Bathurst Street, a short distance north of Queen Street, and in 1858 he built a splendid house on it, which he called "The Hall." Frederick Cumberland designed it. Cumberland was at the time also building his own house Pendarvis on St. George Street at College, and Sherborne Villa for T.G. Ridout and the three houses were quite similar.

Casimir's property extended from Eleanor up to St. Patrick Street (now Dundas). It was in the west half of Park Lot 18 originally granted to Simcoe's secretary, Littlehales. The east half was part of the Denison estate of Bellevue. The frontage on Bathurst Street was more than six hundred feet.

The large buff brick house faced west to Bathurst Street and was set back about five hundred feet from the stone gates. One approached it by a sweeping drive lined with chestnut trees. Casimir loved flowers, and he planned beautiful rose gardens near the entrance. At the north end of the property there was a long line of greenhouses, a cow pasture became a deer park, while an enclosure housed pheasants and rare exotic birds. Behind the house were stables and a coach house. Near the vegetable garden was a small brick building with a brick floor, which originally was meant to be a milk house, but which Casimir turned into a fairy tale playhouse for his children. The Hall became a showplace.

In the south end of the grounds were a bowling-green and a large cannon on a platform. Everywhere were marble statues, pergolas, and benches. A charming octagonal arched gazebo contained a large table. For garden parties the table was covered with a fine lace cloth and rare china and silver. Ladies in bustles and trailing skirts and gentlemen in stiff formal clothes were served to the music of a military band.

The Hall in 1896. Alexandra Park now occupies the site of Casimir Gzowski's famous house.

— Ontario Archives

With its cream-coloured brick and cream-painted woodwork, The Hall was pleasantly light in contrast to the heavy, dark look of most Victorian houses. It had two storeys and an unfinished attic. Compared to some mansions of the day, there were not a great many rooms, but all the rooms were large, their ceilings high, and an air of spaciousness prevailed.

Its architecture was high Victorian: narrow, round-headed windows in pairs, two large Palladian windows on the second floor, a glass and wrought-iron canopy extended from the front door, and the square balcony above the door had a delicate iron balustrade. The eaves were wide, the chimneys ornamental, and there was a picturesque wrought-iron cresting on the roof.

The double front door opened to a large vestibule. Double doors led to a huge reception hall with a floor of red, white, and black

The hallway of The Hall. The life-sized statue of Hercules was made of green marble.
—Metropolitan Toronto Library Board

diamond-shaped tiles. Life-sized statues on high pedestals (one of Hercules in green marble) stood about. The wall beside the staircase was crowded with large paintings.

On the left of the front door was the boudoir, as it was called then, but which would be called a sitting room today. Back of this room was the handsome library, from which one descended a few steps to the billiard room, which was also the art gallery. The paintings which lined the walls from floor to ceiling were all numbered, and guests at large receptions were given printed programs that they might identify the various works of art throughout the house.

To the right of the front door was the large formal drawing room with its elaborate crystal chandelier and white marble mantel surmounted by a large mirror in a massive gilt frame. Long windows opened to a verandah.

From the drawing room one could enter the upper part of the octagonal conservatory built on two levels. A flight of steps led down to the lower level, and that side of the house was filled with a wonderful fragrance from the conservatory.

The second door, on the right side of the front hall, opened to the dining room. An interesting room off the dining room was the Blue Room, so called because of its blue wallpaper, blue rug, and blue upholstery. It was really a sunroom, since it had a glass roof and jutted out from the south wall joining the conservatory. In the Blue Room were cases of stuffed birds and other museum pieces. The gentlemen's washroom opened from the Blue Room.

Back of the main stairway were a cheerful breakfast room with a large kitchen, pantries, and servants' dining room. Many servants were necessary because Casimir loved to entertain. There were maids, footmen, gardeners, besides the cook, butler, and coachman.

Casimir Gzowski built harbours, lighthouses, and a great many bridges. He graded and surfaced north Yonge Street to Richmond Hill. He was one of the founders of the Engineering Institute of Canada, and a founding member of The Canadian Society of Civil Engineers. He had wide financial interests: he was President of the London and Canada Loan Company, Vice President of the Ontario Bank, and one of the founders of the Toronto Stock Exchange.

For many years he was President of the Toronto Club and the first President of the Ontario Jockey Club. T.C. Patteson, whose home Mayfield was on Sherbourne Street, and Gzowski brought the Queen's Plate to Toronto. In 1859 the Toronto Turf Club, of which he was President, petitioned Queen Victoria to give a plate for a thorough-bred race in Ontario. A plate, valued at fifty guineas, was given with the royal blessing, and in June 1860 at the Carleton track, now the southwest corner of Keele and Dundas Streets, the first Queen's Plate was run. Twenty years later when the Governor General, the Marquis of Lorne, and his wife Princess Louise were guests at The Hall, Casimir introduced his guests at the Woodbine racetrack, and the Princess presented the Plate donated by her mother.

He was the first Chairman of the Niagara Falls Parks Commission, and it was he who planned the magnificent park system on the Cana-dian side. He filled in much of the Toronto waterfront, making room for wharves and railway tracks. (Later generations, however, would deplore this as spoiling the lakefront.) Queen's Wharf, at the foot of Bathurst Street, became known as Gzowski Wharf. The International Railway Bridge which he built across the Niagara River linking Fort Erie and Buffalo brought him world fame.

He had a great zest for life. He loved music and was President of the Toronto Philharmonic Society for several years. Many famous musi-cians were guests at The Hall, where they delighted special audiences. He was also a patron of sports, being particularly interested in lawn bowling. He was honorary president of the Ontario Bowling Associ-ation for eight years, during which time many lawn bowling contests were held on The Hall's smooth lawns.

Gzowski was President of both the Dominion Rifle Association and the Toronto Rifle Association, and several times took Canadian teams to England, at his own expense, to compete at Bisley. He donated the Gzowski Cup for rifle competition in Canada, a trophy still awarded today.

In 1879 he was appointed honorary aide-de-camp to Queen Vic-toria, with the rank of Colonel of Engineers. The tall, broad-shouldered Casimir was a magnificent figure in his scarlet and gold uniform, whether in Ottawa or as host at the elaborate social functions

Casimir Gzowski and his family in 1855 on the front steps of The Hall.
— Ontario Archives

at the Gzowski home. Prime ministers, governors general, and members of the royal family were entertained at The Hall in lavish, old-world style.

Besides his other interests, Gzowski was a member of the Senate of the University of Toronto for nearly twenty years. He was a staunch Anglican, a warden of St. James Cathedral, and supporter in the founding of Wycliffe College. In 1881 he entertained the delegates of the Evangelical Conference.

In 1890 he was knighted by the Queen at Windsor Castle for his valuable services to Canada.

The Gzowskis had five sons and three daughters. Two sons died in infancy, and Casimir, born in 1847, was the only son who survived his

Casimir Gzowski, an exiled Polish nobleman, was one of the most romantic figures of nineteenth century Toronto. Above, in 1872, when he was fifty-nine years old.

— Ontario Archives

father. Lady Gzowski was president of the Young Women's Christian Association in Toronto.

On August 24, 1898, Sir Casimir Gzowski died at The Hall. His daughters had all married British Army officers. Lady Gzowski, with her son Casimir and his wife, the former Mary Bell of Buffalo, and their ten children, continued to live at The Hall. In 1904 the property was sold to the City of Toronto for $65,000 and Lady Gzowski moved with her son and family to a house in Rosedale called "Clovelly."

The Hall was demolished, and the seven-acre site became a public park.

There is a brass memorial to Sir Casimir on the east wall of the nave of St. James Cathedral, erected by the officers and men of the Toronto garrison. There is a fine statue of him in Victoria Park, Niagara Falls, Ontario, and in Toronto a small lakefront park at Sunnyside is called Sir Casimir Gzowski Park, where a starkly modern concrete monument, designed by a Polish sculptor, was erected as a centennial project by the Polish community. Symbolic railway tracks radiate from the massive memorial, built to resemble one of the many bridges the Polish engineer constructed. A bronze bust of Gzowski stands in the open centre of the monument, and glass cases contain his magnificent scarlet and gold uniform, medals, a silver goblet, and a copy of the Gzowski genealogical chart. A model of the International Bridge with a bound copy of his notes and plans for it are on display. A tall, slender light above the monument, visible for miles, symbolizes the lighthouses built by him.

In 1963 the Gzowski name was added to the rolls of the National Railroad Hall of Fame in Portland, Oregon, which at that time contained only eighteen names. In the same year a Canadian commemorative stamp was issued, honouring Gzowski.

Alexandra Park now occupies the site of The Hall. The once exclusive neighbourhood has deteriorated, and the beautiful gardens contain swings, wading pool, swimming pool, and winter rink. New Canadians of diverse origins enjoy the park in the grounds once so well graced by one of our most distinguished new Canadians, the Polish exile Casimir Stanislaus Gzowski.

Oaklands

1859-

In the early days of York only one or two styles of architecture were considered suitable for a gentleman's residence. This accounts for the similarity of Bishop Strachan's Palace, Judge Boulton's Grange, and Chief Justice Campbell's home. But forty years later when John Macdonald built Oaklands on the Avenue Road hill, the up-and-coming Victorians built what pleased them. There can be no greater contrast than between Oaklands, Casimir Gzowski's The Hall, and William Thomas's Oakham House, all built within a year of each other.

John Macdonald was born in Perth, Scotland, in 1824. He came to Canada in 1838 when his father's regiment was stationed here. The regiment was called home but John remained. He learned the rudiments of business as a junior clerk in a Gananoque wholesale firm, then became a salesman in Macfarlane's dry goods store in Toronto. The clerks all lived in, and the young Presbyterian, influenced by a Methodist fellow clerk, was planning to enter the Wesleyan ministry when he became very ill. John went to Jamaica, recovered there, and returned to Macfarlane's. He abandoned his theological plans and decided to open his own business.

In 1849 he opened a small dry goods store on the west side of Yonge south of Richmond Street. All important stores and wholesale businesses were then on King Street. Yonge Street, by comparison, was a back street with a few taverns, a scattering of modest dwellings, and many vacant lots. John was laughed at for establishing himself on

Oaklands, as it was in 1897, the Victorian fantasy of Senator John Macdonald.
— Toronto Board of Trade, 1897

Yonge so far north of fashionable King Street, but he chose it because of the low rent. He did not know that this was to be the first blow to the supremacy of the then principal thoroughfare. A few others timidly followed, then more made the move, until Yonge Street became the retail centre of the city.

In spite of the depression of the 1850s and the sneers of the King Street merchants, the little store prospered. John had a flair for advertising. He took out large newspaper space, wrote amusing verses, and attracted customers with shrubs and flowers.

In 1850 he married Eliza Hamilton, but she died soon after their second daughter was born.

John opened a wholesale business on Wellington Street, dealing in dry goods, carpets, and oilcloth, which became the largest in Canada. He was the first to introduce departments and to send buyers to Britain and Europe. His success contributed to the growth of Toronto as the commercial centre of Canada. People called him "the merchant prince."

In 1857 he married Annie Elizabeth, only child of Dublin-born Samuel Alcorn, a wealthy Methodist wholesaler. They had five sons and five daughters.

In 1858 he bought thirty-five acres on the east side of Avenue Road (then called College Avenue) in York Township. The land stretched from modern Cottingham Street up to St. Clair Avenue and extended eastward nearly to Yonge Street. South of it were vacant lots and a few market gardens. There was not a brick house on College Avenue north of Bloor Street.

Between 1859 and 1860 John built a medium-sized brick house on the brow of the hill and called it "Oaklands" because of the oak trees on the grounds. In 1862 the name of College Avenue north of Bloor was changed to Avenue Road and in the next thirty years the address varied from York Township to Yorkville to Deer Park, and Cottingham Avenue to Avenue Road to its present address of 131 Farnham Avenue.

Oaklands is unique. No doubt John Macdonald's Highland blood accounts for its site on the hilltop. Although built near Avenue Road the approach for many years was from Yonge Street, along a lane (now Cottingham Avenue) gradually ascending the hill past the pasture and around to the north of the house. A wooden bridge on tall trestles spanned the ravine on the east side. So picturesque was the bridge and setting, a commercial photographer made a stereoscopic view of it which became very popular.

Originally Oaklands was a two-storey, buff brick house with a slender octagonal tower rising from the ground at its southeast corner. The tower had three rooms one above the other, and a tall, conical roof with

John Macdonald (1824-1890) was one of Canada's great merchant princes. He shared his wealth by giving to many charities, and he loved parties. The baronial great hall of Oaklands held the motto: "Through this wide open gate none come too soon, none return too late."

— Ontario Archives

a weathervane. There were four windows in the front of each storey and a centre entrance through a square porch. East of the house, behind a cedar hedge, were kitchen gardens. One whole acre was devoted to strawberries and asparagus. Large stables and a coach house were northeast of the house. Macdonald was a keen horseman and a member of the Toronto Hunt. He was always well mounted.

The view from Oaklands to Lake Ontario was magnificent, and John claimed that with binoculars he could see Brock's monument at Queenston.

In 1863 he was elected to the Assembly as a Liberal for Toronto West. After Confederation he was defeated, then re-elected in 1875, but, when Sir John A. Macdonald returned to power in 1878, defeated again. He then retired from politics.

By the 1870s dormer windows were cut in Oaklands' steep roof, giving more third-floor bedrooms. A large new tower — square and taller than the first — appeared on the north side. With its steep, conical roof it dominated the façade and only its oriel window saved it from looking like a firehall.

A new wing was added to the west side and a new front entrance opened on the north side. An 1888 photograph shows Oaklands from the southwest. The many-gabled addition has a verandah with Gothic arches formed by slender columns, and a balcony. The bargeboards display exuberant fretwork and there is fancy iron cresting on the roof ridge, and weathervanes or finials on all pinnacles.

A later view of the north face of Oaklands shows the same fretwork and a High Victorian verandah and balcony at the west end. The square bay at the north end of the west side has a crenellated battlement at second-floor level, with the Macdonald coat-of-arms above the windows. The stone carving shows an ancient galley surmounted by a mailed fist clutching a dagger. A gory legend tells that an early Clan Donald chieftain and a neighbouring clan both claimed a large island. It was agreed that the two chiefs would row to the island, and the one whose hand first touched the shore would own it. Macdonald was losing the race, so he chopped off his hand, hurled it to the shore, and won the island.

As strips along the east and south edges of the property were sold, a new entrance was made from the south. Alcorn Avenue (Mrs. Macdonald's maiden name) was laid out as the new southern boundary, a gatekeeper's lodge was built, and gateposts with conical tops similar to the towers guarded the entrance.

The interior of Oaklands was very fine, and much remains unchanged. The wide oak front door, with rectangular lights on sides and top in clear leaded glass, opens to a vestibule panelled in oak. The same fine wood was used throughout the house, perhaps because of the name; also, of course, it was suitable for the interior of a castle.

The great hall, forty-six feet long, was truly baronial and a perfect setting for the famous Macdonald hospitality. The wide staircase beside the north wall, with heavy balustrade of carved strapwork, is unchanged. Opposite the broad landing is a tall stained-glass window with the motto, "Through this wide open gate none come too soon, none return too late." Each of the five hall doors has a flat hood, carved to match the elaborate hall woodwork.

The Macdonald children enjoyed Oaklands' towers, scanning the horizon for Indians or feuding clansmen. The north tower had a tiny room, reached by narrow, twisting stairs, ascending steeply from the second floor. In later years when her daughters were married and far away in mission fields or military posts, Annie Macdonald used the quiet tower room to write her letters. Today the stairs are blocked.

In 1887 John Macdonald was made a senator, the only Liberal ever appointed senator by Sir John A. Macdonald. Although political enemies, they were personal friends.

John shared his wealth. He endowed scholarships, was a generous benefactor to many Methodist churches, and gave numerous Sunday school picnics in the dell north of Oaklands called "The Dish." He supported missions, Lord's Day Alliance, and The Temperance League. When the Salvation Army had enemies he defended it; when the government withdrew its grant from the old General Hospital, he came to the rescue in memory of a daughter who died young. As Governor of Victoria College, he supported the federation of the colleges which resulted in the University of Toronto. (He acquired thirty-seven miniature silver trowels, souvenirs of cornerstones he had laid.)

In 1890 he died. His widow and family lived on at Oaklands for about fifteen years. The three eldest sons were in the family business, another was a master at Upper Canada College.

In 1904 the City of Toronto bought four and one half acres in the southeast corner of the property for $13,320. This little park, known as Cottingham Square, shows how far east Oaklands once extended.

In 1905 the McCormick estate bought Oaklands, and a new entrance was made from Farnham Avenue, now the northern boundary. Cyrus McCormick had improved and produced the reaper invented by his father, revolutionizing farming methods. He died in 1884 but his company expanded into the International Harvester Co. Mary Virginia, his daughter, grew up in a grand Chicago house, accustomed to musical evenings and a profusion of exotic flowers. When she moved to Oaklands she renovated the house and imported rare trees and shrubs. Linden and lime trees adorned the steep slopes where Macdonald children had coasted, and new flower gardens were planted north of the house.

She built an impressive stone porte-cochère at the front entrance and added a bowling alley in the southeast corner of the house. And, of course, she modernized the plumbing.

Miss McCormick shunned publicity. She had a private Negro orchestra which entertained small, select groups. Uninvited neighbours invented strange stories about life at Oaklands.

In 1931 the castle built by the Methodist merchant was bought by the Christian Brothers who had founded De La Salle School for Roman Catholic boys. The property was ideal for a school. They kept the name, and the school became "De La Salle College Oaklands."

The Brothers used the house for classrooms only until the new school opened in 1949. Few alterations have been made to the interior, and handsome fireplaces are not boarded up as in so many converted mansions. The greatest change was a partition built across the great hall where the wide archway had been. The new wall is panelled in fine oak, indistinguishable from the earlier woodwork. The room created on the south side contains the former hall fireplace on its east wall, with a high, intricately carved oak mantel. This room with its bay window was the bursar's office until the drawing room was converted to a beautiful chapel. The office then became the sacristy.

Oaklands became a comfortable home for the Brothers. The former library is now a games room, with billiard and ping-pong tables. The bowling alley, conservatory, and early one-storey wing in the southeast corner were removed and a new wing built which became a staff dormitory and garages. Air conditioners, television sets, and new stall showers do not detract from the dignity of the old house.

With its gables, towers, and gingerbread, its iron cresting and its finials, Oaklands looks a little quaint, but it is one of the finest examples of Victorian domestic architecture in Ontario. Its like will not be built again.

Pendarvis
1860-

The sign in front of 33 St. George Street proclaims it to be Cumberland House, but before that it was Baldwin House, before that Maplehyrn, before that Government House, but originally it was Pendarvis.

The house was built by Frederick Cumberland. Of Cornish descent, he was born in London in 1821 and became an architect and engineer. In 1847 he moved to Toronto. Here he designed many fine buildings — St. James Cathedral, the central part of Osgoode Hall, the Normal School, and University College, whose beautiful main door has been the delight of generations.

In 1859 Cumberland bought a lot at the northeast corner of College and St. George Streets for £1,495 from William A. Baldwin of Mashquoteh, who had acquired it from his brother, the Honourable Robert Baldwin of Spadina. It was part of Park Lot 14 which their mother, Phoebe Baldwin, had inherited from the Elizabeth Russell estate. Robert Baldwin had recently opened St. George, Russell, and Willcocks Streets through the property.

Cumberland called his home "Pendarvis," Cornish for "meeting place" — a prophetic name. It became the centre of fashionable gatherings — a garden party for the Prince of Wales, later Edward VII, who visited Toronto in September 1860, was held here when the house was barely completed.

Pendarvis, said to be one of the finest urban dwellings in the country, is a harmonious mixture of architectural styles. It is similar to Sherborne Villa and The Hall, which Cumberland also designed. Heavy eaves and long horizontal lines contrast with lofty chimneys, curved bays, and vaulted dormers. Conspicuous on the ridge of the high slate roof and around the central parapet is the cresting of wrought-iron maple leaves.

The original front door (now the back door) has an oval of cut glass in the upper half. The stone porch has two stone Doric columns. The wide reception hall, heart of the house, extends the full length from east to west, and is seventy-two feet long! The tessellated floor is now carpeted. The coffered ceiling has blue panels divided by borders of fruit and foliage in high relief moulded plaster. The frieze, cornice moulding, and the ceiling plaster work would be overwhelming if the hall were not so large. (The ceiling is fourteen feet high.) The six panelled mahogany doors are superb — each is forty-four inches wide. All hall doors have high semicircular hoods in carved wood, a pleasant contrast to the rectangular panels of ceiling and walls.

The fireplace on the south wall of the hall has square brown tiles on the floor and sides, with a vertical panel above each end of the wooden mantel. These moulded plaster panels have fruit and corn in the design; the one on the left also has a sculptured beaver. Thus Pendarvis uses both the maple leaf and the beaver in its decoration — surely a very early use of these Canadian motifs.

The dining room, now called Pendarvis Lounge, occupies the northeast corner of the main wing, across from the drawing room. Eric Arthur, author of *Toronto, No Mean City*, says it is the finest Adam room on the continent. It is considered an architectural gem. About forty feet long, it has soft, olive green walls and pilasters, a moulded cornice, and intricate wood carving around doors and windows. The fireplace is an alcove on the north wall — of black and white Ontario marble — and is extremely handsome. There is a single window on each side of the fireplace and there are three windows in a deep bay on the east wall. A china cabinet of four sections, built into the west wall, is more than eleven feet wide.

The wide stairway ascending on the north side of the centre of the hall has heavy, carved balusters, huge newels, and right-angled turns.

Pendarvis in 1886, just after the Cosby family bought it. At the time it was considered to be one of the finest town houses in Canada.

— University of Toronto Archives

It is lighted by a lovely domed skylight above the second floor. The skydome is of frosted glass, except for a pattern outlined in chartreuse.

The third floor, which was the nursery, has small clerestory windows of rich ruby and gold stained glass.

The rooms in the basement, where there was a large billiard room, brought the original total to thirty-three. To give an idea of its size, when St. Stephen's Church burnt down in 1865, the congregation met in Pendarvis for a whole year while the church was being rebuilt.

Cumberland was a man of many talents. He was Chief Engineer of Ontario's first railway, the Ontario and Simcoe, and Managing Director of the Northern Railway.

He represented Algoma in the Ontario Legislature and was a member of the Dominion Parliament. He was founder and first commanding officer of the 10th Battalion of Volunteer Militia Rifles (now the Royal Regiment of Canada), and was aide-de-camp to several Governors General. He helped found the Royal Canadian Institute and was President of the Toronto Cricket Club and the Ontario Jockey Club. Considered one of the best orators of his day, he also found time to write an informed column in Egerton Ryerson's *Educational Journal*. Cumberland was an all-around man in the true Renaissance spirit. Although he practised architecture in Toronto for only fifteen years, his talent and output were so outstanding that he made a lasting contribution to the city. He died at Pendarvis in 1881. His widow remained in the house for three years, then moved to a smaller house in the University grounds a little to the northeast. Two lots, each slightly more than one hundred feet wide on the north end of the property were then sold, reducing the frontage on St. George Street to 390 feet.

In 1884 the house was bought by Alfred Morgan Cosby for $33,250. Cosby, of Welsh descent, was manager of the London and Ontario Investment Company and Commanding Officer of the 48th Highlanders. In 1870 he had married Clara Worts.

Colonel Cosby changed the name of Pendarvis to "Maplehyrn," "hyrn" being Welsh for corner. He built a beautiful conservatory in the southeast corner, which has since been removed. The Cosbys also entertained frequently and lavishly, the layout of the house making it ideal for large gatherings. At this time the address had become 200 College Street.

In 1900 Cosby died. Mrs. Cosby lived there until 1905, when she sold the property to Walter Beardmore, a leather merchant and brother of George Beardmore of Chudleigh on nearby Beverley Street. It was probably about this time that the south verandah with its slender wooden pillars and awning roof was replaced by a large verandah with tall Doric columns and a flat roof with a classical cornice.

In 1912, when Government House at King and Simcoe Streets was demolished to make way for railroad tracks, the Ontario Government leased Maplehyrn as a temporary residence for Lieutenant Governor Sir John Gibson. In 1914 Sir John Hendrie succeeded Gibson and occupied Pendarvis, or Maplehyrn, or Government House (as it was then called), for one year until Chorley Park in Rosedale was ready for occupation.

Frederick William Cumberland (1821-1881), Cornish born engineer and architect.
A man of many talents, he sat in both the Ontario Legislature and the Dominion
Parliament, was founder and commanding officer of the 10th Battalion of Volunteer
Militia Rifles, one of the best orators of the day, and a respected columnist in *The
Educational Journal*.

— Ontario Archives

Mrs. Beardmore returned to the house and stayed until 1919, when the Ontario Government again leased the house and financed Vet Craft Shops for vocational training of disabled veterans.

Twice Pendarvis was in serious danger. Early in 1923 American developers secured an option to the property with the intention of building an apartment building. When word got out, pressure was exerted, the option was allowed to lapse, and the University of Toronto bought the house and land from the Beardmore estate for $210,000. The University took over the house, changed its name to "Baldwin House" at the request of the Baldwin family, and handed it over to the Departments of History and Political Economy.

Baldwin House was really a misnomer, as it led people to think that the Baldwins had built it, or had at least lived there. Generations of students believed that it had been the home of the Honourable Robert Baldwin, when, in fact, he had been dead for two years when the house was built. Although the Baldwin family had owned the land, no Baldwin ever lived in Pendarvis.

The downstairs rooms were not greatly altered, being used for lectures. Upstairs, the head of the History Department held graduate seminars in the large, sunny bedroom in the southeast corner. Other bedrooms were partitioned to make rooms available for small groups and offices. About this time the conservatory was removed.

In succeeding years Baldwin House became headquarters for other university departments — Law, Mathematics, Business, and, for a time, the University Press. When the Wallberg Chemistry Building was built on College Street in 1947, occupying the entire frontage, the address of Baldwin House was changed to 33 St. George Street.

The second crisis was in 1958. The university was looking desperately for room to expand. It was decided to raze Baldwin House to make way for the new Galbraith Engineering Building. Fortunately, Dr. Frank N. Walker and others interested in early Toronto history heard of the plan and went to President Sidney Smith, who had not realized that Baldwin House had been built and occupied by the architect of University College. By an ingenious plan, the historic house was saved. The Forestry Building, adjacent to Baldwin House on the north, was put on rollers and moved 250 feet north! The Galbraith

Building was then built on the site of the Forestry Building, and old Pendarvis, now completely hemmed in by high, modern buildings, lived on. It could hardly be seen except its western front, but it was saved from the wreckers, although denuded of its verandah.

In 1960 students and Rotarians began fund-raising for a new home for Friendly Relations with Overseas Students. In 1965 the University offered Baldwin House and during the next two years the Rotary Club undertook the monumental task of restoring it. At a cost of $220,000 and under the supervision of Professor Eric Arthur, it was done. Partitions were removed and a replica of the first verandah built, although there was no room to replace the conservatory and porte-cochère. Windows were altered to the way they had looked originally, with many small panes of glass and new shutters — exactly like the originals. The roof, eaves, and iron-work were repaired, the front door refurbished, carpets laid, and woodwork painted. New rooms for activities were created in the basement, two tables for table tennis installed in the old billiard room, a work room for processing silk screens set up, and a coffee shop and recreation rooms completely converted the old cellar regions.

Today the exterior is as nearly 1860 in appearance as possible, although the ugly black fire escapes at the back and the television tower on the roof strike a jarring note.

In November 1966 the International Student Centre opened in Pendarvis. Today, university students from other lands congregate here and use its many facilities. Swarms of eager young people — black, white, yellow, and brown, many in turbans, robes, or saris — meet here, gaining a better understanding of each other.

Pendarvis, "the oldest, largest, and most historic house on the University of Toronto campus," is once more "a place of meeting."

Glen Hurst

1866-

Glen Hurst still stands, part of Branksome Hall, a girls' private school. It was built by Edgar John Jarvis, born in 1835, the youngest of the twelve children of Frederick Starr Jarvis and Susan Merigold, who had settled four miles east of Oakville. Frederick was the eldest son of Stephen Jarvis and Rachel Starr, United Empire Loyalists. Sheriff William Botsford Jarvis, who built Rosedale, was Frederick's brother.

When Frederick died in 1852 his widow and children, including Edgar, moved to Toronto. The eldest son, Frederick William, built Woodlawn where Jarvis Collegiate now stands.

In 1863 Edgar married Charlotte, daughter of William Beaumont, F.R.C.S., a clever surgeon with only one eye and the first in Canada to use chloroform. He is also noted for inventing a continuous stitch device to repair cleft palates, the forerunner of the sewing machine.

Edgar bought a large tract of land from his uncle William and built his house on it. He and Charlotte stayed at Rosedale while it was being built. The house, finished in 1866, was on a hill above a deep ravine and they called it "Glen Hurst," "hurst" being an old English suffix meaning hillock or knoll.

At that time there were only four houses in the whole area, which was already beginning to be called Rosedale, after Sheriff Jarvis's house. Except for a few fields, it was almost entirely forest.

The original approach was north on Gwynne Street from Bloor Street, crossing a white wooden bridge built by Edgar's uncle in 1853

Glen Hurst in 1877, with the Jarvis family and their governess in the foreground.

— Mrs. D.J. Fairbrother

where present Collier Street crosses Park Road. Gwynne Street was the first street east of Yonge Street and ran into Park Road which curved to the northeast. When Yorkville was annexed to Toronto in 1883 Gwynne Street became Park Road. The entrance gate to Glen Hurst was on the southeast side of Park Road, exactly opposite the entrance to Rosedale Road. Two square stone pillars, with the name "Glen Hurst" carved on them (now painted over), led to the lane. The lane wound up the steep hillside and emerged behind the house, then circled around in front of it.

The Rosedale glen was delightfully secluded. Its hills were covered with huge trees where lovely wild flowers, especially wild roses, bloomed in profusion, and birds of many varieties sang and nested. A clear stream ran through the ravine in a southeasterly direction to the Don River. Glen Hurst's setting on a narrow plateau high above the ravine was dramatic and picturesque.

Glen Hurst (it was two words originally) was a buff brick house of three storeys, facing west to Yonge Street. For many years there was a wide verandah across the front which extended partway along the north and south sides. The sloping roof of the verandah was supported by slender wooden columns. There was no hand rail (that style came later) and the floor was only two shallow steps above the ground. A centre gable, with a carved vergeboard, provided a narrow window in the front of the attic, while dormer windows, at the sides and rear, gave additional light. A square balcony above the front door was reached by the long French window in the upper hall.

Originally Glen Hurst was a large square block with a steep slate roof, with two bays on the south side crowned by gabled roofs and three gables on the rear or east side. All the windows were large; those on the second floor had slightly rounded heads and coloured glass in the upper sections. All had outer shutters to keep the sun from fading carpets and wallpapers, and those on the ground floor had folding inner shutters which could be closed and locked for greater security and warmth. The deep embrasures of the windows are evidence of the great thickness of the walls, just as the deep doorways throughout the house indicate thick inner partitions.

The wide front door has bevelled glass insets in a Gothic pattern and is flanked by narrow Gothic windows. A large vestibule, with handsome double doors with leaded, coloured glass, opens to a wide hall extending through the house to a door on the east side. The moulded plaster cornice is elaborate and the ceiling is slightly coved. The mahogany baseboard, two feet high, matches the fine doors of the hallway. Obviously the joiners who moulded the woodwork were master craftsmen.

Edgar Jarvis owned a great deal of land in Rosedale and pioneered its development into an exclusive residential area. Success in his real estate business came slowly, as the area was remote from the city, it was difficult to keep servants there, and access was limited.

For some time he warned the Yorkville Council that the wooden bridge on Park Road was unsafe, but the Council took no action. In

Edgar and Charlotte Jarvis and their children. Edgar pioneered the development of Rosedale, but whenever the family fortunes declined, as they did from time to time, Charlotte gave endless piano lessons to help keep the family together.

— Mrs. D.J. Fairbrother

1872 the bridge collapsed and a cabdriver and his horse were killed. The bridge was not rebuilt, but the ravine at that spot was filled in. There is still a dip in the road there. Edgar built a private bridge to the north of Bloor at Huntley Street. His new approach to Glen Hurst was north on what became known as Bridge Street (later Huntley Street and now part of Mount Pleasant Road) to Elm Avenue and west into his house.

At the new upper entrance to the Glen Hurst grounds, he built tall stone pillars with "Glen Hurst" carved on them and large ornamental iron gates and fence, which are still there. The new entrance was a great improvement over the lower one, as the steep, muddy hill from Park Road was difficult in bad weather. The address, however, remained as Park Road.

Glen Hurst 165

The Huntley Street bridge later acquired notoriety as "the Suicide Bridge," when numbers of despairing individuals solved their problems by jumping from it to the ravine far below. Exploring boys and Sunday strollers alike walked across the bridge to look over it in hopes of glimpsing remnants of clothing caught on the trees below.

Edgar and Charlotte had ten sons (two died as children) and three daughters. Glen Hurst was an ideal setting for lively, growing children. The boys trapped muskrat and occasionally mink in the weeds at the stream's edge. With the gardener, Edgar and the boys planted hundreds of trees along the new streets, which he called Maple Avenue and Elm Avenue. He named several streets for his family: Rachael for his grandmother, Beaumont and Beau for his wife and eldest son, Percy and May for his twin children, and Edgar for himself.

Charlotte was both musical and literary. Under the pseudonym Rosedalia, she wrote delicate verse, a volume of which, *Leaves from Rosedale* was privately printed in 1905. One of the most charming poems, "My Coach and Eight," relates how during a period of retrenchment, when the horses had been sold and she had been ill, her eight sons pulled the family carriage to give her an outing.

Years later at Charlotte's funeral in 1927 the clergyman read this poem aloud as her eight sons carried her casket from the church.

Edgar built a number of fine houses in Rosedale, which he sold. On the west side of Glen Road he built Norcastle, a turreted mansion, the first one to use Credit Valley Stone — it set the fashion for a generation. When Henry Darling bought Norcastle he renamed it "Hillcrest." In 1905 it was bought by Sir Albert Gooderham who changed the name to "Deancroft" in memory of his mother, Harriet Dean. This impressive house, with its beautiful interior panelling and spacious grounds, was for years one of the showplaces of Rosedale. In 1935 it was demolished and several undistinguished houses replaced it.

In 1876 Edgar built a mansion on Beau Road (later 152 South Drive) which was purchased by Sir Edmund Osler, who called it "Craigleigh." This beautiful house, in thirteen acres of ground, was demolished in 1932, and part of the estate became a park.

Opposite Norcastle, on the east side of Glen Road at the approach to the north iron bridge, Edgar built for himself a house of white brick,

MY COACH AND EIGHT

One day I rode in a car of state,
 And never was queen more proud than I,
I was drawn in triumph by horses eight
 To a neighbor's house a half-mile nigh.

For sickness had left me weak and lame,
 And hard times had left no horse in stall
I "needed change, and it were a shame
 That I should not have it," said they all.

My boys ran off without more ado,
 And into the relic of days gone by
The brave fellows harnessed two by two,
 Nor wanted a whip to make them fly.

Indeed 'twas enough to make folks stare,
 And even the dogs flew out to bark,
But I in my glory did not care,
 And to them all it was but a "lark."

Arrived at the neighbors', all turned out
 To view my steeds as they took a rest,
And at once agreed, without a doubt,
 My equipage was of all the best.

Then into the house, where all was light,
 And truest friends gave me welcome rare,
Till I scarce could tell which was more bright
 The light or the laughter rippling there.

They left me there, and the evening passed
 As a happy dream, too quickly o'er;
The time for farewells had come at last—
 My coach and eight stood before the door,

With blazing torches our way to light,
 Whilst lamps and boughs made the carriage gay
And the silent hush of the summer night
 Gave place to cheers as we drove away.

Dear boys! whatever befall me yet,
 Or gloom or sunshine to me betide,
Till memory fail, I will ne'er forget
 The pride and joy of my one state ride.

backing on the second ravine. Resembling a fairy-tale illustration, it was called "Sylvan Tower" by the Jarvis family, who moved into it in 1881. In 1933 it was demolished.

To open the new area in the north and east of Rosedale, Edgar had to build a bridge over the first ravine. In 1881 he built the first iron bridge on Glen Road at a personal cost of $30,000. He brought both the engineers and the iron from Scotland. Each purchaser of property in the area was given the right to use the private bridge. The new bridge, almost six hundred feet long with a plank floor spanning the deep ravine immediately north of Bloor Street (which at that time extended only to Sherbourne Street, some distance west of Glen Road), was considered a marvel when it opened. It connected the south end of Glen Road to the new section of Rosedale.

As soon as Edgar opened his private bridge, all the residents of the area began to use it, and every delivery cart found that it was a short cut to the northeast. Edgar unsuccessfully tried to get the City to buy the bridge. Then, in an attempt to recoup some of his expense, he set up barriers and charged a ten-cent toll to all but pedestrians. Eventually one angry neighbour, Maunsell Jackson of Drumsnab, drove his carriage and four horses at a furious gallop across the bridge and smashed the barriers — declaring that he would henceforth pay the toll in that manner! A musical comedy feud developed, which did not end until the City of Toronto (which had annexed Rosedale in 1887) paid Edgar Jarvis $10,000 for the bridge, a fraction of what it had cost him. This bridge is still in place, although in 1925 a landslide damaged its supports and in 1950 vehicular traffic was forbidden. Today it is a pedestrian bridge and leads to a tunnel under Bloor Street.

The Jarvis fortunes began to decline. To help keep the family together, Charlotte gave endless piano lessons, with the latest baby usually in a basket on top of the grand piano.

Eventually Glenhurst, as it was now spelled, was sold to Bernard B. Hughes who with his brother Patrick had a successful wholesale business in dry goods, carpets, and millinery.

In 1892 Glenhurst was sold to John Waldie, President of the Victoria Harbour Lumber Company. Soon afterwards the address of Glenhurst became 75 Park Road and the Rosedale Ravine Drive was its southern boundary. Each succeeding owner retained the name of Glenhurst.

In 1920 Sarah, widow of John Waldie, sold Glenhurst to Colonel Frederick H. Deacon, a member of the Toronto Stock Exchange and President of the Canadian National Exhibition.

In 1948 the Glenhurst property, now only six acres, was sold to Branksome Hall School, which was flourishing in several large houses on Elm Avenue at Huntley Street. Its main building was the former Hollydene at 10 Elm Avenue. The principal of this private boarding and day school for girls was an enterprising lady, Dr. Edith M. Read. Glenhurst was converted to classrooms for grades five to eight.

The verandahs were removed, leaving a large porch on both west and south sides. All mantelpieces were ripped out and the fireplaces were covered over and painted to match the walls. Fire escapes were installed, and the crumbling pinnacles of the tower were shorn from their corners. Some of the chimneys, now unnecessary and in poor condition, were taken down. The south door became the front door and a gymnasium was built in a long, narrow addition to the east of the house. The house itself, however, was not structurally altered.

In 1950 Toronto's first expressway was completed. Huntley Street was widened and extended to connect Jarvis Street with Mount Pleasant Road. The name "Huntley Street" was dropped, and it was henceforth part of Mount Pleasant Road. Rosedale's quiet seclusion ended, and the Branksome Hall girls found a highway running down the middle of their grounds. Several times a day the indomitable Miss Read stood on the busy road holding a stop sign to allow her girls to cross. The city installed traffic lights, but Dr. Read did not rest until she persuaded the Council to build an enclosed, elevated walk where the girls could cross in safety. It is called "Read Walk."

Today Glenhurst is called "Readacres," in honour of Dr. Read. In 1958, when she retired, she had been principal of Branksome Hall for more than fifty years!

The sparkling stream where the Jarvis children trapped muskrat and mink now runs underground in a sewer, and the wild trilliums, hepaticas, and roses have been dug up and carried away, but Glen Hurst is still flourishing in its useful new career.

Josephine Burnside was Timothy Eaton's eldest daughter. To house her superb collection of eighteenth century furniture and art, she transformed Bellevue into one of the most beautiful houses in Toronto.

— Eaton's Archives

Bellevue

1866-

Beautiful Bellevue still stands, but no one can see it because, except for part of its south wall, it is hidden within a larger and later house at 49 Clarendon Avenue.

The property was originally part of Lot 23 in the 2nd Concession from the Bay, a two-hundred-acre lot running from modern Bloor Street to St. Clair Avenue. It was part of Admiral Augustus Baldwin's estate, Russell Hill. Gradually the Baldwins sold off pieces of land until Samuel Nordheimer owned most of the west side, north of Davenport Road (Glen Edyth) and Edmund Gunther owned much of the east section.

In 1866 Edmund Gunther, a jewellery importer from Germany, bought about twenty-two acres from the Honourable John Simcoe Macaulay's widow. The property extended along the south side of modern St. Clair Avenue between Poplar Plains Road on the east and modern Warren Road on the west. It tapered southward to a point at the base of the Davenport ridge. The Gunthers called their estate "Bellevue."

Bellevue was a white brick house on the brow of the hill facing east to Poplar Plains Road. A long driveway between tall pine trees and hawthorn hedges curved to the house from the lodge gates opposite the end of the present Edmund Avenue, ending in a circular driveway. Edmund Avenue was a short street running between Avenue Road and Poplar Plains Road.

The original Bellevue in 1866, when it was owned by Edmund Gunther and his musical daughters, seen in the foreground.

— Mrs. R. Bethune

Poplar Plains Road was originally a steep, winding trail made by Indians travelling between Lake Ontario and their village north of modern Eglinton Avenue. In winter it made an exciting and dangerous bobsled run for the neighbourhood children.

Well proportioned Bellevue consisted of a wide, main section with long windows and a chimney at each end and a rear wing which extended farther south than the front. A wide verandah ran across the front and along both north and south sides. The walls were two feet thick. All windows had strong inside shutters, which could be locked.

To the right or north side of the wide front hall was a pleasant breakfast room with a door on its east side to the back hall. On the south side of the house were the drawing room, dining room, and music room, all with long French windows opening to a verandah, smooth lawns, and flower gardens. All had fine crystal chandeliers and the charming music room had long French mirrors.

Beautiful Bellevue in 1965, from the rear, looking relatively unchanged since Mrs. Burnside's death in 1943.

— Ellen Russell

A side door on the north side of Bellevue opened to the back hall, where a curving staircase led to family bedrooms above. The back hall led to the wing which held kitchen, pantries, servants' quarters, and a large conservatory where grapes, apricots, and out-of-season plants were grown.

Southwest of the house beyond the high hedges were extensive kitchen gardens, a bake house, stables, coach house, and other outbuildings, while north of the house were orchards, fields, and woods.

In 1890 the Gunther family sold the north part of the property as far as St. Clair Avenue, then just a sandy track. In 1902 the remaining land, by then in Deer Park, a suburb of Toronto, was sub-divided.

Gunther's daughters were talented musicians who had studied in Dresden, Germany, where the eldest had been a pupil of the famous Franz Liszt. Because of their admiration for Liszt and Schiller, they chose these names for the new streets through Bellevue's property. The driveway leading to the house remained a private road for those who bought lots there. Called "Clarendon Crescent" now, it is still a private road.

In 1903 Henry James Bethune, grandson of Bishop Alexander Bethune, bought Bellevue and two acres of land for $10,500. Henry, an inspector and shareholder of the Dominion Bank, had married Laura, daughter of Chief Justice Thomas Moss, and was living on Beverley Street. This house seems to have been included in the purchase of Bellevue, as one branch of the Gunther family occupied it for some years.

The Bethunes' six sons and one daughter found the nearby hills, woods, and pond idyllic. Bethune made no structural changes in Bellevue, but when in 1911 they moved to Oriole Road, they took Bellevue's fine crystal chandeliers with them.

Bellevue was bought by Edward Hume Blake, eldest son of the Honourable Edward Blake, once Premier of Ontario, who had had a most distinguished political career, and Margaret Cronyn, daughter of the first Anglican Bishop of Huron.

Hume Blake (he dropped the Edward) was born in 1860, and became a barrister in the firm of his father and uncle. In 1889 he married Georgina, daughter of Alexander Manning, who, like the Blakes, was of Irish descent. Manning was a wealthy contractor with varied interests ranging from the presidency of the North American Land Company and of the Toronto Brewing and Malting Company to the ownership of the Grand Opera House. He was Mayor of Toronto in 1873 and 1885.

Blake immediately renamed Bellevue "Humewood," which had been the name of his father's house on Jarvis Street (now the Red Lion Inn) and of his grandfather's home on the present Humewood Drive. The original Humewood, home of his ancestors, was in County Wicklow, southeast of Dublin, Ireland.

Hume added a wing to the west side. It contained a handsome library on the south side overlooking the garden with a billiard room back of it and two bedrooms above. The addition extended to join the brick stables and contained a kitchen, pantry, and servants' quarters on the north side. The house now had six family bedrooms. The north entrance was enlarged and became the front door with a new porch. The house thus acquired an east-west orientation, facing north to Clarendon Avenue.

The grounds were delightful. Trees of the original forest provided shade and a high hedge along the south and east borders provided privacy. A grass tennis court and a lovely pear tree, reaching to the top of the covered verandah, is still vividly remembered by Mrs. C.H. Wright, Hume Blake's only daughter.

The large living room, or drawing room, was almost thirty-five feet wide on the garden side and nearly twenty-three feet deep. It had two French doors opening to the wide, old fashioned verandah.

Hume Blake was an enthusiastic horseman. With his two sons and daughter he followed the hounds with the Toronto Hunt Club. Rows of sterling silver trophies on a large mahogany table proclaimed their expertise. He even erected a series of practice jumps on the property, which the whole family enjoyed.

When Blake retired from legal practice he became President of the Manning Cold Storage Company.

In 1928 the Blakes moved across the road to a new house. They sold Humewood to Mrs. T.D.M. Burnside. Mrs. Burnside (Josephine) was the eldest daughter of Timothy Eaton and a director of the T. Eaton Co. Born in St. Mary's, Ontario in 1865, she had moved with her parents to Toronto in 1869. In the early 1890s she married Mr. Burnside, who preferred English country life to Canada. They lived in England and travelled a great deal. A daughter, Iris, was born in 1895, and a son, Alan, in 1898.

After some years, Mrs. Burnside separated from her husband, but continued to travel widely. A connoisseur of fine furniture, glass, and china, she amassed a large collection of eighteenth century furnishings and rare paintings.

A dreadful tragedy befell her in 1915. She and her daughter were travelling to England for one of Iris's periodic visits with her father. They sailed on the ship *Lusitania*. It was torpedoed and sunk by a German submarine off the coast of Ireland. The twenty-year-old Iris was drowned, but Josephine, by a freakish accident, was saved. She was blown up a smokestack; then spent a harrowing eight hours in a lifeboat. She was so covered with oil and soot everyone thought her to be a crew member. Some time later they noticed her jewellery. Her companion, Miss Mattie Waites, was drowned too.

In 1927 Mrs. Burnside returned to live in Canada, and began to search for a suitable home where her large collection of period furniture and objets d'art could be properly housed. She bought Humewood from the Blakes for $145,000 and engaged her favourite nephew, Henry Burden (son of her sister Margaret who had married Charles E. Burden), to remodel and enlarge the house.

The architects, Burden and Gouinlock, given a free hand and a generous budget, spent nearly a year transforming the house. The old ridge roof was raised, a fine bracketed cornice added, and the final result was such an outstanding example of the late Georgian style of architecture that in 1931 it won first prize in an exhibition of the Ontario Association of Architects in the Domestic Exteriors over $75,000 class. In true eighteenth century spirit all the important rooms — drawing room, living room, dining room, and library — have a commanding view of the gardens with their rare shrubs, long arbours, and formal arrangements of walks and flowers, and it is the close relationship between the house and beautiful landscaped grounds that is the greatest attraction of the property today.

The architects won the second prize in the Domestic Architectural Details class for their design of the entrance gates. A brick wall, with an iron railing above it and with stone urns in classical style surmounting the brick pillars, encloses the front of the property. The curving driveway passes under a large stone porte-cochère with round arches. All the exterior decoration is in cut stone, which harmonizes well with the grey brick walls.

The square entrance hall was dominated by the fireplace (since removed) on the east wall, which had once graced a fine London home — its mantel being of statuary marble designed by the English architect, Sir William Chambers. The central panel, carved in lively detail, showed a bear knocking over a beehive. The carved plaster ceiling and deep cornice of this hall and the cross corridor into which it opens were inspired by this fine mantelpiece.

Mrs. Burnside's elegant drawing room. The walls were covered with cream brocaded silk panels and were a fitting background for the delicate French antique furniture.
— Eaton's Archives

The walls of the new drawing room were covered with creamy, brocaded silk panels — a fitting background for the antique French furniture. The window curtains were of similar brocade but slightly darker. Delicate Louis XVI armchairs, a lady's writing desk with tortoise-shell and brass veneer, and other period pieces graced the room. An elaborate crystal chandelier in the lofty ceiling drew the eye, and one could almost imagine that satin-clad courtiers had just left this beautiful salon.

Mrs. Burnside employed a large staff to care for her beautiful house. There were four resident gardeners to look after the grounds and the large conservatory in the southwest corner. She did not, however, entertain a great deal, giving the impression she had created this Georgian gem of a house chiefly as a suitable background to display her superb eighteenth century furniture, paintings, and objets d'art.

In 1934 Mrs. Burnside gave the Eaton home on the northwest corner of Lowther Avenue and Spadina Road to the I.O.D.E. for their headquarters. A red brick mansion with a large conservatory, stained glass windows, and a Moorish room, it was prominent in an area of Victorian mansions. In 1965 it was torn down, and a tall apartment block replaced it.

In 1937 Mrs. Burnside's son Alan died. Five years later she turned over her valuable Clarendon Avenue property to the Canadian Mothercraft Society for a nominal sum, again demonstrating her generosity.

In December 1943 Mrs. Burnside died.

The house became a training centre for well-baby care, and the Mothercraft Society, in gratitude, named it "Burnside." On the whole, few alterations were made, only such internal changes as were necessary to comply with fire regulations. A large room on the northwest side was renovated as a diet kitchen, and the three-car garage became a day-care nursery school. The lovely gardens, with their long arbour, gazebo, and fountains were preserved, and for over twenty years thousands of fortunate babies benefited.

In July 1963 the Canadian Imperial Bank of Commerce bought the property for $350,000 to use as a staff college. The Canadian Mothercraft Society moved into the former quarters of the bank's staff college at 616 Avenue Road. Since then Mothercraft has moved to the home of the late Senator Wallace McCutcheon at 32 Heath Street West.

The third Humewood, alias Burnside, now became the only residential training facility owned by a Canadian chartered bank. The Bank uses the house as a resident and non-resident school to train its accountants and managers.

The Bank still calls the house "Burnside," and has changed it as little as possible. When neighbours heard that the property had been sold, they feared the lovely house would be demolished. Today, however, the exterior is quite unchanged and the gardens are as well maintained as before.

Euclid Hall
1867-

Today the northeast corner of Jarvis and Wellesley Streets is occupied by a tavern restaurant, but in 1866 there was no corner, let alone a tavern, because Wellesley Street stopped on the west side of Jarvis. The following year Wellesley continued eastward and Sheriff Jarvis's house, "Woodlawn" (where Jarvis Collegiate now stands), found itself on the south corner. To the north was open country.

In that Confederation year, Arthur R. McMaster built a large house on the north corner. Born in Ireland, he had joined the wholesale dry goods firm of his uncle, Senator William McMaster, whose summer home, Rathnelly, was on the Poplar Plains Hill. As Arthur prospered he invested in real estate on Jarvis Street.

In 1868 the McMasters moved into their new yellow brick Gothic Revival house with its romantic towers, oriels, gables, crenellations, and unexpected bays. It was the one-of-a-kind type which the later Victorians built to advertise their wealth. Nothing could be more unlike the restraint and symmetry of the earlier Georgians. Fantasy had become the keynote.

A white picket fence bordered the property and a large brick carriage house and stable stood in the rear.

In 1882, after McMaster died, Hart Massey, the fifty-nine-year-old president of Massey Manufacturing Company, bought the house. Hart was born near Cobourg, Ontario, the son of Daniel Massey, a farmer who loved to repair his and his neighbours' crude implements. In 1847 Hart married Eliza Phelps, an American. Daniel moved to Newcastle and began making implements. Soon Hart became superintendent of the foundry, then a partner. Under his management and his imaginative advertising campaigns the firm grew rapidly. In 1856 when Daniel died, Hart became president.

In 1870 Hart moved to Cleveland, leaving his eldest son Charles as vice president. The plant moved to Toronto in 1879, and three years later Hart returned, resumed control, and bought the McMaster house, with its twenty-six rooms and seventeen fireplaces. Remembering their happy years on Euclid Avenue in Cleveland, the Masseys decided to call their new home "Euclid Hall."

At that time Jarvis Street was a pleasant tree-lined boulevard, eighty feet wide. It had become a good address and mansions sprouted on either side of it.

Euclid Hall has been altered so much that it is difficult to determine exactly what its interior was like originally. Some features, however, are unchanged. The porte-cochère's fine stone carving and the flowers and leaves carved in stone around the bow windows flanking the front door are still there. The double front door with its coloured glass is unchanged, and the stained-glass windows on the north side of the wide reception hall are doubtless original, as are the exterior marble columns between pairs of upper front windows and the lovely oriel window jutting out on the north side of the hall.

Hart's famous grandson, Vincent, son of Chester Massey and his wife, Anna Vincent, remembers in his memoirs the delightful fountain in the centre of the front hall where goldfish swam in an octagonal glass pool. He writes that the house was crammed with fascinating souvenirs, mementoes of the world travels of Hart's children. There were models of buildings from Bible stories, Arab costumes, a tiny Swiss chalet, a magic lantern, African spears, mummies, Roman helmets, and, at one time, some live monkeys in an enclosure in the garden.

Hart and Eliza had four sons and one daughter. The house seemed always filled with grandchildren. Chester lived next door, and his sons Vincent and Raymond were always underfoot in Euclid Hall. For some

When Euclid Hall was built Jarvis Street was a pleasant tree-lined boulevard, eighty feet wide. It had become a good address and mansions sprouted on either side of it.
— Raymond Massey

time the children of Charles, who died in 1884, lived with their grandparents. When Walter married Susan Denton in 1888, the young couple occupied a suite in Euclid Hall for two years. They moved to a house of their own across the road, but were constantly at Euclid Hall. At that time Lillian and young Fred Victor were still at home.

Hart, the stern Methodist patriarch who forbade cards, dancing, alcohol, and tobacco in Euclid Hall, was a devoted family man. He adored his only daughter and his obsessive devotion so restricted her social life that Lillian did not marry until after her father's death. At the age of forty-two she married a pious widower, John Treble.

The Masseys have been generous to Toronto. In 1894 Hart made two magnificent gifts. In memory of his youngest son who died at the

Hart Massey (1823-1896), a stern Methodist patriarch who forbade cards, dancing, alcohol, and tobacco in Euclid Hall, gave Massey Hall and the Fred Victor Mission to Toronto — two magnificent gifts.

— Massey Ferguson Archives

age of twenty-three, he founded the Fred Victor Mission. Soon afterwards he gave the non-profit Massey Music Hall to Toronto in memory of his eldest son, Charles Albert. Designed by Edward Lennox, who had recently completed City Hall and who was to be the future architect of Casa Loma, the Hall was "to assist Toronto's religious and musical programs." Most of the famous musicians and lecturers who appeared at Massey Hall were first entertained at Euclid Hall. Hart Massey was also generous to Victoria University and the Toronto General Hospital.

Following Hart's death in 1896 the bulk of his estate became The Massey Foundation which built and endowed Hart House in the University of Toronto.

Euclid Hall, with a large sum of money to maintain it, was left to Eliza Ann and afterwards to Lillian. When Lillian married she assumed control of the family home and continued to occupy it with her husband. Eliza, who had seen three of her sons grow to manhood and die young, lived until 1908. Lillian became a widow the following year.

Lillian made a number of changes in Euclid Hall. Although it remained a strictly Methodist home, she added colour and glamour. She moved the massive walnut staircase from the centre to the north side of the wide reception hall, where it is now approached beneath a Gothic arch.

She installed an elevator and redecorated all the rooms, adding bathrooms with king-size marble basins and tubs. The bathroom off the master bedroom, a former dressing room, even had a fireplace, possibly the only bathroom in the country with one. She built a sunporch above the porte-cochère and installed a pipe organ between the music room and the reception room.

Her most dramatic change was to convert a small room on the main floor into a Moorish room. A square archway with tall green columns divided the reception room from the Moorish room. It was a period when the rich were introducing Oriental furnishings into their homes; in Lillian's case, the Moorish motif had captured her fancy. The multifoil, cusped arches, invented by the Moors, appear in Massey Hall too, but in a Victorian house they had a particularly exotic air. The coloured brass, the small, low tables inlaid with mother-of-pearl, and slim pillars with capitals coloured bright green, gold, red and blue, made Euclid Hall's Moorish room mysterious and glamorous. A rich Oriental rug covered the floor, wicked-looking scimitars hung on the walls, and the mahogany couches were covered with dark blue plush piled high with cushions. Guests would not have been surprised if turbaned slaves had appeared in the horseshoe-shaped arches, dimly lit by coloured, hanging lamps. (Old Torontonians may recall that the Timothy Eaton house on Lowther Avenue also had a Moorish room.)

In 1901 the Duke and Duchess of York, later King George V and Queen Mary, visited Toronto and stayed at Government House. In later years it was said that they had stayed at Euclid Hall. The legend persists to this day, although there is no basis for it.

Lillian also was a philanthropist. Her desire to see girls get a sound domestic education resulted in the building of the Lillian Massey School of Household Science and Arts at the southeast corner of Bloor Street and Avenue Road, her gift to the University of Toronto.

Lillian died in 1915, and Euclid Hall was loaned to the Government to be used as a Convalescent Home for severely wounded soldiers.

The Military Hospital left in 1924, and the following year the house was bought by Thomas Ryan. When it was sold, Vincent Massey took the charming fountain from the front hall and installed it in his home, Batterwood Park, near Port Hope.

Tommy Ryan was a colourful sportsman who had invented five-pin bowling but had neglected to patent it, thereby losing a fortune. The coming of Prohibition had ruined his hotel business, and he decided to go into antiques and auctioneering. Euclid Hall became Ryan's Art Galleries. The fine old furniture, paintings, silver, and Oriental rugs which he displayed showed to advantage in the elegant rooms. He called his own private quarters the "Royal Suite," which may have started the rumour that the Duke of York had slept there. Tommy Ryan was not a man to waste good advertising.

A true showman, he exploited the Victorian mansion to the fullest. Ryan's Art Galleries were rented by various organizations for decorous fund-raising activities. It became popular with university students for their dances and the young people found the fragrant conservatory and the dimly lit Moorish Room very romantic.

A corner of Lillian's Moorish Room.

— Panda Associates

In 1927 Ryan rented space to a new organization called C.F.R.B., which broadcast many entertainers from a studio in Euclid Hall.

During the Depression, ten years later, Ryan sold a strip of land along the south side of the property to an oil company. A garish service station mushroomed there, and a large portion of lawn was paved. This meant the removal of the beautiful conservatory, an operation which left the south side of the house pitifully maimed. About this time, too, a fashionable dancing school opened in the former bedrooms on the third floor.

Ryan's Art Galleries continued to occupy Euclid Hall until about 1961. During the later years Ryan had rented space in the house to various architects, engineers, geologists, mining syndicates, the Registered Nurses' Association, Canadian Players' Foundation, a cosmetics company, the Canadian Association of Health, and other assorted tenants.

Gradually the fine old house declined. In 1962 it housed the Voltaire Restaurant, operated by Douglas Campbell, the soap-box orator who paraded with "Ban the Bomb" signs and was in constant trouble with the Health Department.

The once splendid Euclid Hall reached the nadir of its degradation when a coffee-house called "Uruhu" (Swahili for freedom) set up shop there. The house swarmed with beatniks and hippies. Speculators who had bought the house ignored the filth, and were not concerned with the abuse the house suffered. They were merely waiting for someone to buy it, demolish the house, and build an apartment building. In fact, they nearly gave up hope of a good sale and considered pulling the house down and converting the land to a parking lot.

Fashionable Jarvis Street, once the residence of the rich and powerful, had undergone a complete metamorphosis. In the lower part of the street, fine old houses had been converted to cheap rooming houses and sleazy hotels with unsavoury reputations.

Traffic increased when the trees were removed, as the grassy boulevards were sacrificed to widen the road. Most of the occupants of the big houses had long since moved to Rosedale, Forest Hill Village, and latterly, Bayview. Some of the mansions were occupied by institutions, other had been replaced by tall apartment blocks. It was the end of an era.

In 1963 Euclid Hall was rescued by Julius Fine, the flamboyant operator of the successful Gaslight Restaurant in Yorkville. Delighted with the house and its bygone Victorian elegance (he said its elegance was bygone nearly beyond recall), he took a thirty-year lease on the property. A year and a half and a reputed quarter of a million dollars later, Fine had completely renovated the house and restored it to its early opulence. When he opened for business in January 1964, a big sign above the porte-cochère said, simply "Julie's." In the newspapers it was often referred to as "Big Julie's."

Fine made few structural changes. In converting the former dining room to its new use, it was necessary to remove the wall where the fireplace was, but the change was made skillfully.

The pious Baptist who built the house and lived there for twelve years and the strict Methodist who succeeded him for the next seventeen would have been horrified to find a cocktail bar in the former music room, and scantily clad females serving drinks in the master bedroom.

Late in 1975 Julie's Mansion closed its doors. Old Euclid Hall once more underwent extensive alterations. Today it houses one of the Keg'n' Cleaver chain restaurants.

Mayfield
1871-1966

John A. slept here. Sir John A. Macdonald not only slept here, he and his family actually lived here for a year.

Mayfield was built by Thomas C. Patteson. Born in England in 1836 and a graduate of Eton and Oxford, Patteson came to Canada in 1858 and became a lawyer. He was captain of a famous international cricket eleven and founder of the Ontario Jockey Club. In 1867 he became Assistant Provincial Secretary for the new province of Ontario, and in the same year he married Marie Jones of Port Hope.

In 1870 Patteson bought three acres of land on the east side of Sherbourne Street, immediately north of Carlton and extending back to Bleecker Street. At that time Sherbourne was a mere sandy lane with only one house north of Carlton Street and open country north and east to Parliament Street.

Patteson paid $3,000 for the land. He immediately began to build his house on it and used some materials salvaged from a cottage on Government House property which was being torn down, as Government House had burned. It was these old bricks and timbers in the basement which led a well-known authority to state nearly a century later that the house had been built around an 1840 cottage.

The house was large and rambling, of greyish brick, three storeys high. It contained fourteen rooms, not counting those in the basement. It was not of any particular architectural style and may only be called Victorian. A single gable in the middle of the front broke the

Mayfield, just before it was torn down. Built in 1871 by Thomas Patteson, editor and manager of *The Mail*, for sixty-seven years it was the home of the Trees family who saw the once elegant neighbourhood degenerate into a near slum.

— *The Globe and Mail*

horizontal lines; the windows were all round-headed. A pair of narrow, round-headed windows on the third floor in the gable matched a similar narrow pair in the north and south dormers. A small closed-in wooden porch with peaked roof duplicated the line of the gable and protected the front entrance. A neat picket fence bordered the front.

In 1872 *The Mail* was founded as the Conservative newspaper to counteract *The Globe*'s influence. T.C. Patteson became editor and manager. During his years with *The Mail* he was very close to Sir John A. Macdonald who frequently stayed at the Patteson house. They had many discussions regarding *The Mail*'s policy. Under Patteson's editorship it became one of the leading newspapers in Canada, and his editorials paved the way for the Conservative victory of 1878.

T.C. Patteson excelled as a correspondent. His by-line was "Quartz," the result of a printer's error. The printer, seeing "Quartz" to be the last word in one of Patteson's articles, thought it a signature. Patteson adopted it and made it famous.

Since 1872 Sir John A. Macdonald had been toying with the idea of retiring to private life and settling in Toronto. In 1875 he rented the furnished house of his friend Patteson for one year, at $100 a month. It was a temporary arrangement while he looked for a house to buy. While in Patteson's house (then 373 Sherbourne Street), he held many conferences, busily planning a Conservative comeback. He was then living down the Pacific Scandal, but already had new plans for the railroad which would unite Canada. In the early summer of 1876 the Macdonald family moved to their new house on St. George Street near the present Knox College.

Soon after Sir John moved out of the Sherbourne Street house, Patteson sold it to Samuel Trees. Two years later Patteson resigned from *The Mail* and became Postmaster of Toronto.

Samuel Trees was an Englishman with a successful business which manufactured buggy whips, saddles, and harnesses. He was a city alderman and treasurer of the St. George's Society. Trees gave the name "Mayfield" to the house, and he furnished it with imports from England and fine local Jacques and Hay furniture. The Trees family was to live in Mayfield from 1877 to 1964.

Samuel Trees was associated with Sir Henry Pellatt in bringing hydro-electrical power to Toronto, and in about 1901 Mayfield became one of the first Toronto houses with electricity. Chandeliers designed for gas were wired. In all other matters regarding the house, however, Mr. and Mrs. Trees resisted change. When Mrs. Lucas, a daughter, left Mayfield in 1964, she told reporters she believed the house had never even been redecorated or any of the furniture replaced since her parents first furnished it.

From the outside Mayfield looked huge, but the rooms were not as big as one would expect. Hallways were so broad and rooms so cut up into irregular shapes they lost their spaciousness. The large square front hall had a gracefully curved stairway and a lofty ceiling with a border of moulded plaster work. Shining bronze statuary, huge paintings, and clusters of swords vied for attention with the potted palm

Mayfield's large square front hall had a graceful curved stairway and a lofty ceiling. The furnishings were unmistakably Victorian.

— Ontario Archives

and majestic grandfather clock. Rich maroon velvet curtains hung by large wooden rings from heavy oak poles and covered doorways.

The room to the right was called "The Red Room." Everything in it was red. The deep-piled carpeting and the patterned wallpaper were deep red, the chairs and sofas rich, red brocade. Oriental touches were everywhere. Although The Red Room was so crowded one could hardly move among the small tables and large chairs, to the Victorians it was just right. The fireplace had a carved wooden mantel, back to back with an exactly similar one in a smaller sitting room in the rear. Both rooms had wide French windows on the south side which opened to a long verandah, lovely gardens, and huge old trees.

Mayfield 191

The room on the left of the hall was dominated by an intricately carved, mirrored Chinese altar, flanked by small shelves which held Oriental objects in delicate porcelain, ivory, and carved teak. Mr. Trees was a world traveller and brought home the many treasures that overflowed all horizontal surfaces. The ceiling had an elaborate plaster centrepiece with a cherub's head at each end, the same as in the front hallway. Above the white marble mantelpiece was a gilt-framed mirror. It reached to the ceiling.

An archway from the hall led to a smallish library, where the fireplace was on an angle in the north corner. Unexpected angles and asymmetry were popular in Victorian houses.

In 1918 Samuel Trees died. In 1933 Mrs. Trees died, leaving her daughters Charlotte and Edith to maintain the house. With the help of several servants they kept it in good repair, furnished exactly as it had been for over eighty years. In 1964 Edith, the last survivor, went into a nursing home and the Toronto Parking Authority bought the property. The grounds had shrunk to two-thirds of an acre as the Carlton Street frontage had been sold off long ago. The Authority planned to demolish the house and use the land, valued at $35,000, as a parking lot.

The furnishings were put up at auction, and a huge walnut bed with a carved headboard reaching to the ceiling, which might have been the one Sir John slept in, brought only $325.

In October 1965 transients broke into the house and their careless smoking started a fire. And it was only then — when Mayfield had stood empty for a year, when its interior was charred beyond recognition and filled with broken plaster — that a clamour arose to save the old house.

Several times The Toronto Board of Control set the date for Mayfield's demolition and several times a reprieve was granted while a group, hastily organized as the Fathers of Confederation Historical Foundation, tried to raise money to buy it and convert it into a museum and library. But they could not raise enough and finally time ran out. In the spring of 1966 Mayfield was demolished and a municipal parking lot now occupies the site.

Chudleigh
1871-

Few Toronto houses have had as checkered a career as Chudleigh. The once-elegant mansion at 136 Beverley Street on the northwest corner of Dundas was built by George L. Beardmore, a solid Canadian of English extraction, for his own residence. He would have been astonished if he could have foreseen that seventy years later his home was to be seized by the Canadian Government as alien property!

George was born in Chudleigh in Devonshire. When he first came to Ontario he worked in Thornhill as a clerk in a tannery. Later he moved to Hamilton where he had his own tannery and wholesale leather business. Soon after the birth of his sons — Walter in 1849 and George in 1851 — Beardmore moved to Toronto. In addition to his expanding leather interests, he became President of Dominion Lumber Company.

About 1870 he acquired a large lot on the west side of Beverley Street in the fashionable neighbourhood of The Grange. There he built his house and named it "Chudleigh" in memory of his English birthplace.

Chudleigh occupies a lot two hundred feet on Dundas Street and one hundred and fifty feet on Beverley Street. It is built of buff-coloured brick in the Second Empire style with a mansard roof covered by slates. It is a large house of some thirty-five rooms, once surrounded by a brick wall of the same dirty grey as the house. Originally this wall, eight feet high, had jagged bits of broken glass scattered along the cement coping. In one of its later lives, the bricks of the façade and the front wall were painted white. This may have smartened the house's appearance at the time, but today the white paint is peeling in a depressing manner.

To the left of the front entrance an iron gate in an arched opening in the brick wall led to a secluded lawn and garden. The high wall shut out all the sights and most of the sounds of busy Dundas Street.

The large coach house of the same brick is now joined to the house by a storeroom, and back of it is the original brick stable which once accommodated many horses.

A square porch, supported by two Doric columns and two pilasters with a flat protruding roof, protects the front entrance to the right of centre. A wide door with semi-circular fanlight opens into a vestibule, leading to a small square hall. Through a curved archway one then enters the main hallway. The wide stairway with its large newel posts sweeps upwards to the right in a long, graceful curve.

Chudleigh contains three complete sets of staircases. Halfway up the main stairway is a wide landing with a large, arched window in the centre facing north with a smaller arched niche on each side. The stairs to the basement are as wide, and curve as gracefully as the main stairway. In the basement there is a large walk-in vault with combination locks.

George Wahlen Beardmore, who carried on his father's leather business, never married, and lived at Chudleigh all his life. Among his many interests horses came first. He was an expert judge and a tireless rider. He was Master of Fox Hounds of the Toronto Hunt Club from 1893 until 1931, which is something of a record. During 1893 he kept the hounds at home, which indicates how rural the Chudleigh neighbourhood was. About seventy hounds were kennelled there. Until the late 1890s it was common for a meet to begin in Queen's Park and spread northward.

George Beardmore loved to entertain and, after his mother's death, his sister, Mrs. Henry Fisk (who in 1916 had moved next door), frequently acted as hostess. Ladies in their lopsided riding habits, and gentlemen in hunting pink often met there after a good day's sport.

Originally Chudleigh was the large rural home of George Beardmore who as late as 1893 kennelled seventy hounds on its grounds on the corner of Dundas and Beverley Streets.

— Ellen Russell

In 1934 George Beardmore died. Chudleigh stood empty for three years, then became the Italian Government's consulate. It became "Casa d'Italia" — an Italian flag flew from the tower and the Italian coat-of-arms stood above the front door. The old house changed. The walls, which for so many years had echoed to horsey talk, now heard animated Italian at the numerous receptions given by the Consul.

In the south end of the basement terrazzo tile was laid on the floor and on the walls to a height of four feet. Colourful Italian coats-of-arms were displayed in the floor, honoring Il Duce and the Italian monarchy equally.

When World War II broke out, Chudleigh became suspect. At this time a number of wealthy Italian Canadians were interned for their efforts to send money and horses to Rome. Chudleigh, with its many

George Beardmore (1851-1934), businessman, bachelor, and avid horseman, lived in Chudleigh all his life.

— Ontario Archives

rambling rooms and communicating doors, provided an ideal setting for possible cloak-and-dagger plots. The Canadian Government moved swiftly and confiscated Chudleigh as alien territory.

For several years the house again stood vacant, prey to weather and vandals. In 1943 the Royal Canadian Mounted Police took it over as their local headquarters.

Chudleigh remained a barracks for the R.C.M.P. until 1961, when the Italian community bought the property and returned it to the Italian Government. Italy presented the house to the local community which needed an education centre. It was renamed "Villa Vista." Volunteer workers toiled for a year to clean and refurnish the old house.

It was a big undertaking. The years of vacancy and neglect had left a mess of fallen plaster, broken glass, and warped floors. Fixtures had been smashed and the woodwork was dingy. Although no one believed rumours that the Mounties had stabled horses in the house, people wondered how it could have become so dilapidated.

Finally, in 1962, the house was presentable, and COSTI, the Italian Community Technical Training Promotion Centre, officially opened. Partitions had been put in the larger rooms and school desks installed in the former drawing room and conservatory. The white cross, Roman eagle, and fasces in the terrazzo floor in the basement were almost hidden by shavings and heavy lathes of the new carpentry shop. In addition to English language classes, there were shops to teach upholstering, picture-framing, and other useful trades. A large coin machine for dispensing soft drinks made its appearance in the hall leading to the old dining room.

Today Chudleigh is undergoing yet another renovation — it is being converted back to becoming the Italian Consulate. Chudleigh, the stately old dowager is still at work.

Glen Edyth
1872-1929

Glen Edyth was once the finest private house in Toronto, perhaps even in Canada.

In January 1871 Samuel Nordheimer bought twenty-five and a half acres of Russell Hill property for $8,100 from the Honourable Robert Baldwin's heirs, and in 1872 he built his house on it.

The property was V-shaped and Poplar Plains Road was the eastern boundary. The apex was just north of the Canadian Pacific Railway tracks north of the junction of Dupont Street and Davenport Road. There was a level crossing there where today the road goes under the railway.

Samuel Nordheimer was born in Bavaria, Germany, in 1824, the son of Jewish parents. With his older brother Abraham he emigrated to Canada when he was fifteen years old. They founded a music supplies company which became the biggest of its kind in Canada. They manufactured organs, pianos, and other instruments, and their store on King Street sold the latest music sheets, as well as tickets to all musical affairs.

In November 1871 Samuel married Edith Louise, daughter of barrister James Boulton, who was a brother of D'Arcy Boulton of The Grange and Henry Boulton of Holland House. The blonde twenty-five-year-old Edith was considered one of the most beautiful women of the day. Eleven children later, she was still beautiful.

Glen Edyth was built by Samuel Nordheimer for his wife, the former Edith Boulton, the most beautiful woman of the day. Eleven children later, she was still beautiful.
— Mrs. Philip Kerrin

Before the marriage, a European-style agreement was signed in which Samuel granted the land to Edyth and covenanted to erect a dwelling house on it furnished to the minimum amount of $25,000; to transfer it all to Edith for his life and after his death as long as she remained his widow.

Nordheimer built the mansion on the ridge above Davenport Road, not far east of the Spadina property boundary. He called it "Glen Edyth" in honour of his bride and the lovely glen nearby. It stood on the north side of modern Glen Edyth Place. It was in the township of York, a long way from the city limits at Bloor Street.

The entrance gate was north of the railway crossing and was guarded by an unusual lodge. Built of brick with quaint, timbered gables, it was in two parts which joined overhead. The gardener lived in one half, the coachman in the other, and carriages drove through the opening in the middle. The road turned left, passed a duck pond and waterfall where Boulton Drive now joins Poplar Plains Road, and branched into two approaches to the house. The left fork, now Glen Edyth Drive, was used by carriages. It was longer and easier, winding gradually up the hill and crossing three rustic bridges over the stream which flowed down the ravine towards Bloor Street. The right fork went up through the glen and climbed a steep ascent to join the other road near the top before it circled in front of the house.

The beautiful wild valley northwest of Spadina House, running down to Poplar Plains Road, was known for many years as the Nordheimer Ravine. It was popular for hikes and picnics. (This lovely spot has now been raped by bulldozers to make way for a sewer and a controversial expressway.)

Glen Edyth was built of buff brick. It contained about thirty-five rooms including the basement. A staff of a dozen servants was required to keep it going, and there were always two men on the box when the carriage drove out.

A large part of the roof was flat. An ornamental iron balustrade surrounded it, permitting people to walk there and enjoy the spectacular view. There were two towers — the one high above the front entrance had a glass roof with an iron railing around it.

The large porte-cochère had a balcony above it with an ornamental wooden railing and at intervals, urns. Verandahs and porches of various shapes appeared on all sides in European villa style.

In 1877 *Illustrated Toronto Past and Present* said, "It is, with the exception of Sir Hugh Allan's residence in Montreal, the most superb in all the Dominion."

The main entrance hall had a large fireplace and was lighted by an open lightwell which rose to the top floor where there was a large glass dome with four coloured lamps for gala occasions. An ornate brass grille surrounded the well on the upper floors.

The lodge gate to Glen Edyth was guarded by a two-part lodgehouse. The gardener lived in one half, the coachman in the other. The road wound gradually up the hill and crossed three rustic bridges before it circled in front of the house.

— Metropolitan Toronto Library Board

On the east side of the hall were the small drawing room and the large, formal drawing room which opened to a ballroom, all sumptuously furnished. At a Glen Edyth ball guests found many nooks and alcoves for romantic tête-à-têtes. A bright breakfast room was off the ballroom. Dazzling crystal chandeliers illuminated all the larger rooms, and steam heat was supplied to ornamental radiators with marble tops by a vast coal-burning furnace.

On the west side was the high dining room, off which were the billiard room, library, and smoking room. A bathroom, pantry, and butler's room were off a back hall. The pantry had a dumbwaiter which brought up meals from the basement kitchen.

The second floor, known at that time in continental fashion as the first floor, contained Mrs. Nordheimer's boudoir or sitting room, bedroom, and dressing room, and two other bedrooms with connecting bathrooms and dressing rooms.

On the west side was the schoolroom, connected to Mr. Nordheimer's bedroom and bathroom. A staircase ran down to his study.

The grounds were on the same magnificent scale. Large gardens with ornamental trees, formal flower beds, and delightful paths were similar to the private parks which surrounded English estates. There were two summerhouses and an orchard with fruit trees and grape vines.

The stables with five box stalls, two coach houses with groom's quarters, and harness room were in the rear. There was also a kitchen garden, greenhouse, icehouse, cowshed, and pigpen. The family vault was placed in the side of the bank overlooking the glen. Life in the Glen Edyth establishment must have been much like the "Upstairs Downstairs" television programme, except on a larger scale.

Nordheimer was President of the Federal Bank of Canada and a director of other companies. For years he was President of the Philharmonic Society of Toronto and brought famous musicians to the city.

He was German Consul for Ontario, and an impressive figure in his uniform and decorations. He became an Anglican and a member of St. James Cathedral.

Mrs. Nordheimer was interested in the Children's Aid Society and the Working Boys' Home, and was president of the I.O.D.E. and the Ladies' Branch of the Canadian Red Cross Society. She was presented to Queen Victoria and entertained governors general and visiting royalty. Splendid life-sized portraits of Samuel and Edith hung beside the main staircase. They were painted by John C. Forbes, R.C.A., who executed portraits of King Edward VII and Queen Alexandra.

Both Mr. and Mrs. Nordheimer died in 1912. Their only surviving son, Roy Boulton, a graduate of Royal Military College, continued to live in Glen Edyth until 1924.

Then, except for a caretaker, it stood vacant until 1928. In 1929 it was demolished. The land was subdivided and Glen Edyth Place opened through the site of Russell Hill and Glen Edyth. A large modern house now stands on Glen Edyth's circular drive.

Devon House

1874-

The Cawthra family, "the Astors of Canada," not only contributed much to the financial and social life of Toronto, they also built a number of very fine houses.

The Cawthras were an old Yorkshire family. Over the centuries their name was spelled in a variety of ways: de Caudry, de Caudray, Cathra, Caudrew, Caudrey, Cawdra, Cawdray, Cawdry, Cawdrew, Cawdrey, Cawthera, Cawtherah, Cawtheray, Cawtherey, Cawthray, Couthray, Coutheray, Kawdrey, Kawtherau, Kawtheran, and, in Scotland, Calder.

The ancestor of the Canadian Cawthras was Joseph Cawthra, who sometimes spelled his name "Cawthray." He was the son of Henry Cawthray and Mary Brown (his mother's name presented few problems). Joseph was born in 1759 at Yeadon Hall, Yeadon, near Bradford in the parish of Guiseley. In 1781 he married Mary Turnpenny. There were six sons and three daughters, but only three sons and one daughter survived to accompany their parents to Upper Canada. They arrived in York in 1803, having stayed briefly in Scotland and New York before deciding to settle in Canada. Grace, their daughter, married Alexander Legge, but died without children. The sons — Henry (whose twin brother Joseph had died in England) died unmarried in 1854; William died childless; and John. Of Joseph's nine children only John had a family. Today's Canadian Cawthras are all descended from John, son of Joseph and Mary.

Joseph opened an apothecary shop in York, specializing in patent medicines, but, like our modern drugstores, it was something of a general store. It sold dry goods, shoes, hats, cutlery, watches, tobacco, sugar, coffee, tea, chocolate, needles, bed-ticks, and brandy. Drugstores today may have an even wider selection, but seldom sell bed-ticks. Joseph also dabbled in real estate.

He received a Crown Grant of two hundred acres of land near Port Credit, part of which is still in the hands of descendants. The land is called "Cawthra Lotten" — it was Lot 10.

Joseph's shop did very well, especially during the War of 1812, but it was his youngest son, William, who amassed the great wealth of the Cawthras.

Born at Yeadon in 1801, William married Sarah Ellen Crowther in 1849 (which must have seemed like a further variation of the name). They lived at Jarvis and Bloor Streets while their fine mansion of dressed stone was being built on the northeast corner of King and Bay Streets. The site was historic because the first white child born in York was born in a small house there in 1795. William's house was designed by Joseph Sheard, a fellow Yorkshireman who also designed Trafalgar Castle at Whitby, now the Ontario Ladies' College.

The Cawthra house, built in 1851, has been called the finest town house in classical style ever built in Canada West, and was on a par with the best townhouses in London. Perfectly proportioned, with Corinthian columns, it was famous for its sumptuous interior. Many legends grew up concerning its rich appointments. One widely believed story was that the butler removed a solid gold doorknob every evening from the big front door, and replaced it with one of mere silver!

This splendid, classical house later became a bank, but in 1946, in spite of opposition, the building was demolished, an irreparable loss to Toronto. The name of this house is not known, but a grandniece believes that it may have been called "Yeadon Hall."

William died in 1880, childless and intestate, and his brother John's children benefited from his wealth.

John, fifth child and third son of Joseph and Mary Cawthra, was born at Yeadon in the parish of Guiseley in 1789. He married Ann

Devon House today. It was only one of the many fine houses the Cawthra family, the Astors of Canada, built in nineteenth century Toronto.

— Jack Mitchell

Wilson in 1821 and settled at Newmarket, Upper Canada. He was the first representative of the County of Simcoe in the Legislative Assembly in 1828. He had four sons and one daughter. In 1851 John died. Joseph, the eldest son, built Guiseley House in Rosedale. Mary, the daughter, married Dr. Thomas H. Mulock, and one of her sons was William, later Sir William Mulock. William died when only seven years old, and John, born in Newmarket in 1824, built Devon House on Beverley Street. Henry, the youngest, owned Yeadon Hall on College Street.

There were only scattered houses on Beverley Street in 1870, and there was no Dundas Street bisecting it. Because of The Grange, the neighbourhood was fashionable, although still remote. Two years later St. Patrick Street (now Dundas Street) was opened, and George

Beardmore erected his fine house, Chudleigh, at the northwest corner of Beverley Street and St. Patrick.

In 1874 John Cawthra began to build a large house north of Chudleigh, at the southwest corner of D'Arcy Street. The two houses occupied the entire block. Except for the Honourable William Cayley's mansion, The Home, one block to the north, there were open fields stretching to College Street. Even ten years later there were only four houses on the west side of Beverley Street between St. Patrick and College Streets: Chudleigh, Devon House, The Home, and Lambton Lodge, home of George Brown, editor of *The Globe*.

John Cawthra was born in Newmarket, Upper Canada, in 1824, the second son of John and Ann (Wilson) Cawthra. He was the grandson of Joseph Cawthra.

Young John attended Upper Canada College in York, and as a young man founded a wholesale business on King Street East. He retired "with a competence" in 1857, and the business eventually became the Murray-Kay Company. John then founded the Farmers' and Merchants' Loan and Savings Bank, of which he was President until shortly before his death, when control passed to his nephew (Sir) William Mulock.

When he was forty, John went to England to find a wife, preferably one from outside the great cities. He met Elizabeth Jane, daughter of Thomas and Mary Elwell of Devonshire, who was exactly the bride he was seeking. They were married in London and travelled extensively in Europe before returning to Toronto.

When they built their buff brick house at 130 Beverley Street, they decided to call it "Devon House," in memory of Elizabeth's birthplace. John's elder brother Joseph had built Guiseley House in Rosedale, on the southeast corner of Huntley Street and Elm Avenue, and soon afterwards his younger brother Henry bought a house at the southwest corner of College and Beverley Streets which he called "Yeadon Hall."

Devon House was a large, three-and-a-half-storey house, surrounded by a wooden fence. It was in the French Second Empire style, which had become popular in Paris about 1860, and spread to Canada in the 1870s. The style was characterized by a mansard roof, covered by slates (which at Devon House were arranged in a pleasing pattern of three colours), and with dormer windows in the nearly vertical, lower slope of the roof. These windows were invariably trimmed with a wide, curving architrave, and can still be seen in many of the surviving houses in the neighbourhood of Devon House. The cornice of these houses is always prominent, with numerous brackets.

As in most houses in this style, the chimneys of Devon House are above inside walls, an arrangement which led to less heat loss than when fireplaces are built on outside walls.

Devon House had a central hall plan, the entrance being through a closed brick porch, with a semi-circular glass fanlight above the double, outer doors and a similar high fanlight above the solid inner door.

A small greenhouse was on the south side of the house and extensive vegetable gardens in the rear. The large stables and carriage house were of the same grey buff brick as the house. A driveway from D'Arcy Street led to the stables.

The open light well in the centre of the house was unique. A large rectangular skylight in the roof, with sloping sides, provided light for the front halls, which would otherwise have been gloomy. On the outside above this hip-roofed skylight, was a wooden finial carved in the shape of a small urn. Beneath the clear glass of the exterior skylight, the interior ceiling was of coloured glass.

On both the second and third floors the central light well was supported by four slender columns of painted iron, which had spiral carving running their length and which branched at the top into ornate capitals of carved fruit. A strong metal balustrade surrounded the open light well and inevitably attracted children and grandchildren who enjoyed hurling missiles down into the hall below. To prevent the children from leaning over too far in their curiosity to see the formally attired adults proceeding two-by-two like animals into Noah's Ark, from drawing room to dining room, Mrs. Cawthra had a strong wire netting strung across the open light well, on both second and third floors.

Mr. Cawthra had a great fear of fire. He therefore planned his house so that the family bedrooms on the second floor would all have communicating doors. His theory was that if the door opening on the gallery around the light well should be blocked by fire, they could escape through one of the other bedrooms, and find an exit to the hall. Apparently he did not consider what a through draft might do if all doors were left open.

John Cawthra did not enjoy his gracious new house for long, as he died early in 1875. There is a fine window in St. George's Church dedicated to his memory. His widow Elizabeth continued to occupy Devon House for some years. Her daughter Winifred had died in infancy and her eldest son, John Elwell, died in 1886 when he was only twenty-one years old. Her son William Herbert, born in 1867, married Alice M. Beatty in 1897. He was a barrister with financial interests, and he lived with his wife at Devon House until it was sold. Elizabeth's youngest daughter, Ann Mabel, had been born in Lucerne, Switzerland, in 1871. When she married Lieutenant Colonel Agar S.A.M. Adamson, she, her husband, and two sons shared the house. Ann designed and presented to Toronto the drinking fountain in Queen's Park, opposite St. Joseph Street.

In 1890 the number of the house became 150.

About 1910 Mrs. Cawthra built a porte-cochère at the front door, with an elegant glass and iron canopy flaring out above the steps, greatly enhancing the appearance of the façade.

In 1919 Devon House was sold to Henry J. Fisk. Three years later Elizabeth Cawthra died.

Mrs. Fisk was a sister of George Beardmore, the owner of Chudleigh, the large house south of Devon House at the corner of Dundas Street (the name of St. Patrick Street had been changed to Dundas in 1918). The fence between the two properties was removed, and the beautiful lawns and gardens were often enjoyed by the guests of both houses. Mrs. Fisk frequently acted as hostess for her bachelor brother, who had a strict rule that all evening affairs at Chudleigh must terminate sharp at midnight, with the result that his guests, ready or not, had to leave, like reluctant Cinderellas.

Because Mrs. Fisk wished to orient her property towards her brother's house, a great many changes were made in Devon House. One major change involved moving the front staircase from the south to the north side of the house. (It has been said that relocating the stairs was the usual winter entertainment in early Ontario!)

Mrs. Fisk made other changes to modernize Devon House and much of the original moulding around doors and windows was altered.

In 1930 after the Fisks died, the ownership of Devon House passed to George Beardmore. The house remained vacant until 1936, when it was acquired by Arnoldi Hundert, a baker and caterer. Devon House was renamed "New Chudleigh," and the vast basement soon became a busy bakery, with a large kitchen in the northwest corner.

Shortly afterwards the property was purchased by Jewish Community Services, but Hundert Caterers stayed there until the late 1950s, and their part of the house was in great demand for receptions of various kinds. Weddings and garden parties were very popular there, especially in the summer when the lovely grounds could be enjoyed.

About 1953 the central light well, which had made Devon House so unusual, was closed by removing the balustrade around the gallery and extending the floor across the opening, on both the second and third floor levels. A new partition, from north to south, divided the space in two. The old iron columns with their spiral carving may still be seen on the second floor — two in the hall, one in a back hall, and the other in an adjoining room, all looking lost and somehow embarrassed.

When the United Jewish Welfare bought the property from Hundert Caterers, old Devon House became headquarters for the Canadian Jewish Congress, and the offices of the United Jewish Welfare Fund.

The house was cut up into many offices. Partitions were installed in the large rooms, the drawing room on the north side was divided in two, the library became three offices, and most of the fireplaces were covered over. Additional plumbing was installed. The fine hardwood floor of the front hall, which had become scarred, was covered by bright tiles.

In 1962 a new building was given the number 150 Beverley Street. Erected on the southern edge of the property right on the street line, this modern, red brick building strikes an incongruous note, squeezed as it is between the dignified grey brick of nineteenth century Chudleigh and Devon House. It houses three agencies and is called the "J. Irving Oelbaum Centre." The spacious lawns of old Devon House have disappeared under concrete paving which extends to the very walls of the house.

Wychwood
1874-

In 1874 Wychwood looked over the roofs of Toronto far out across
Lake Ontario. A yellow brick house in a Victorian version of Gothic
Revival style, it perched on the brow of the hill high above Davenport
Road, a short distance west of Bathurst Street.

With the advent of soaring skyscrapers and the haze of pollution,
the view has lost some of its charm, although a narrow slice of Lake
Ontario can still be glimpsed. But modern Wychwood has turned her
back to the view and now faces north to a delightful private park. The
address is 6 Wychwood Park.

Wychwood was designed and built by Marmaduke Matthews, an
artist of Welsh descent. He was born in 1837 in Barcheston,
Warwickshire, England. He studied painting in nearby Oxford and in
1860 moved to Toronto. Four years later he eloped with Cyrilda Bernard. Cyrilda's father, Colonel Bernard, pursued them, brandishing
the traditional horsewhip. The young couple fled to the United States,
but several years and babies later they were forgiven and returned to
Toronto. Marmaduke's portraits and landscapes brought in little
money, so he bolstered his income by colouring photographs.

In 1873 Matthews bought ten acres of heavily wooded land on the
outskirts of Toronto, in Lot 26, 2nd Concession from the Bay, for
$4,000 and began building the house which he called "Wychwood"
after Wychwood forest near his childhood home. He patterned the
house to some extent on his ancestral home, Fifefield Manor.

Wychwood today. When it was first built it commanded an unbroken view over Lake Ontario.

— Jack Mitchell

For many years there was only one other house in the area bounded by Christie Street, St. Clair Avenue, Bathurst Street, and Davenport Road. The approach to Wychwood was a steep lane, winding up from Davenport Road east of the house, which then formed a circle in front of the house with a flower bed in the centre.

Wychwood has twelve rooms in two storeys and an attic. The greyish yellow brick is laid in a decorative pattern beneath the eaves. The triangular, peaked upper windows have red and yellow bricks alternating in the projecting label above the top and upper sides. Such brick patterns, said to originate in Ireland and still seen in rural areas of the province, are unique to Ontario. The roof is steep with wide gables at the east and west ends. The chimneys are in pairs, linked top and bottom.

Four years after building the front section of Wychwood, Marmaduke added a wing in the rear with similar although narrower gables at the east and west ends and the same window treatment. Between the steep roofs of the two wings is a section of flat roof. Each wing had its own furnace.

All woodwork in the house is pine. The elaborate moulding surrounding the wide doorways was made in sections and fastened with small, sunken, square-headed nails.

The original dining room was back of the library, and its floor was several inches higher to accommodate the ceiling of the basement kitchen. The dining room was heated by a stove. The early kitchen had an outside door on its east side, where the ground sloped away.

The stable and outbuildings were northwest of the house, with tennis courts on the west side, usually approached from the long window in the "back parlour," with its charming circular steps of old bricks.

Marmaduke's studio was a large room in the northwest corner of the second floor with a skylight thirteen feet high. Eventually his landscapes began to have a modest success, but he lost so much money with unsuccessful inventions that he had to mortgage Wychwood to his son-in-law Ambrose Goodman, who had built a house next door to the east. Cyrilda must sometimes have wondered if her father hadn't been right to object so strenuously to her marriage.

In 1880 Marmaduke Matthews became a charter member of the Royal Canadian Academy of Arts and acted as its Secretary for some years. He was also a founding member of the Ontario Society of Artists, and was elected its President in 1894.

From 1888 to 1898 he spent every summer painting landscapes in western Canada under the patronage of Sir William Van Horne, President of the Canadian Pacific Railway. When the railway bought his paintings and displayed them for advertising purposes, Marmaduke won fame and some prosperity. Although today critics do not regard his paintings as great art, they recognize their value as documentaries.

Marmaduke had a dream of founding a co-operative artists' colony in the beautiful wooded neighbourhood of Wychwood. He and Alexander Jardine bought twelve acres west of Wychwood, where in 1877 Jardine built his home, Braemore Gardens. In 1891, with Agnes

Marmaduke Matthews (1837-1913), artist and builder of Wychwood. He wanted to found a co-operative artists' colony in the neighbourhood of Wychwood, and, although his dream failed, several fine artists have lived in Wychwood Park.

— Metropolitan Toronto Library Board

A watercolour by Marmaduke Matthews titled "Hermit Range, Rocky Mountains." From 1888 to 1898 Marmaduke spent every summer painting landscapes in western Canada under the patronage of Sir William Van Horne.

— Art Gallery of Ontario

Litster, Jardine's mother-in-law, they formed a trust company to sell land to artists and academics, who would build substantial houses around the large pond, formed when Marmaduke dammed up Taddle Creek. This famous stream rises in Wychwood Park and originally flowed down a deep ravine and under a culvert at Davenport Road in a southeasterly direction, erupting periodically into basements and surfacing for a last time east of the University of Toronto library to form the ducking pond for freshmen. It is now lost in sewers on its way to the lake.

Wychwood Park never became the artists' colony dreamed of by Marmaduke, although some fine painters have lived there. George A. Reid, the muralist, and Gustav Hahn, whose Art Nouveau ceilings enrich many Toronto buildings, were the best known. Architect Eden Smith lived in the Park, as did Charles Currelley of Royal Ontario

Museum fame. Sir William Gage built his large Palladian home high on the hill at Davenport Road and Bathurst Street. Gage planned to build a sanatorium there, but his outraged neighbours dissuaded him.

The Park was annexed by the city in 1909, but it is still autonomous, governed by a board of three trustees, elected annually. About fifty homeowners pay city taxes, but do not pay local improvement rates. The community raises and administers funds for roads, water, sewers, and street lighting. Wychwood Park is still a delightful, secluded area of old trees, winding roads, wild flowers, and birds.

In 1913 Marmaduke Matthews died but his wife Cyrilda, son Melville, a school principal, and daughter Mrs. Ralph Pack and husband and daughter Alice, the "baby," lived there for years.

In 1960 Alice, the last survivor, sold the house on its diminished lot to John Wickham-Barnes, head of television music for the Canadian Broadcasting Corporation's English network, and his talented wife, Janet. They found the attic and every cupboard crammed with articles saved by the Matthews's for eighty-five years. They removed the grime and the many coats of paint and varnish until the pine floors, wainscots, door and window frames were restored to a mellow beauty. Because it made the hall dark, they removed the original solid front door to the north entrance, which is now the front door. The drawing room and hallway had been covered by paintings floor to ceiling, and the plaster was deplorable. A dozen coats of wallpaper had to be removed. Mr. Barnes repaired the inch-and-a-quarter floorboards and restored pieces of furniture abandoned in the attic.

The basement kitchen became a billiard and recreation room, while the former dining room above it was converted to a modern kitchen.

Today Wychwood is a warm and gracious home, where the eighteenth and nineteenth century furniture of the present owners finds a perfect setting.

The pond, ravine, and tennis courts are owned communally by Park homeowners. Originally the pond was much larger and held water lillies, wild ducks, and even small boats. In the old days swimming and skating parties were held there. Today the only link to the past is the red carp, descendants of Marmaduke's grandson's goldfish. The grandson, Martin Goodman, emptied his goldfish tank there before he left for the First World War, from which he did not return.

Lambton Lodge

1875-

The massive house on the northwest corner of Beverley and Baldwin Streets is much like its builder, George Brown — austere and dignified. Just as Brown was uncompromising and humourless, his house has no whimsical turrets or cupolas, no romantic balconies. Heavy stone trim above doors and windows and a solid iron fence were exactly right for the man who pounded home his arguments in speeches and editorials with a sledge hammer. His house, like him, has a timeless, dependable air.

George Brown so admired "Radical Jack" Lambton, Lord Durham, whose Report sought to solve the problems which led to the 1837 Rebellion, that he called his house "Lambton Lodge" and sometimes "Lambton Court." Born near Edinburgh in 1818, George came to Toronto in 1842. He and his father started a newspaper; two years later they founded *The Globe* with George as editor. Under his guidance it wielded a powerful Liberal influence.

In 1851 George was elected to the Legislative Assembly. Before long he became leader of the Clear Grits, a somewhat radical wing of the Reformers.

During a holiday in Edinburgh in 1862 George met Anne Nelson, the daughter of a wealthy publisher. George, tall and serious, was ten years older than Anne, a sensitive and cultivated girl. Two months later they were married and were welcomed home in Toronto by fireworks and a huge crowd.

Lambton Lodge and its owner George Brown of *The Globe* were not unlike —
austere, dignified, solid.

— Jack Mitchell

George played a prominent part in the Quebec Conference where his
stern sense of duty overcame his personal antipathies and broke the
deadlock between Upper and Lower Canada. He resigned from the
Government before Confederation and was appointed to the Senate in
1873, and it was his thunderous editorials that were largely responsible for Canada acquiring the vast territory of the Northwest from the
Hudson's Bay Company.

In 1875 the Browns began to build a house. It had to be large
enough for frequent entertaining, yet suitable for family life. For
$5,800 they had bought a lot 388 feet wide on the west side of
Beverley Street. At that time there was only one house between
Dundas and College Streets and they could see The Grange clearly
from their property.

They built a red brick, three-storey house with a mansard roof covered with slates; a heavier version of the French Second Empire style. Coach house, stables, henhouse, cowshed, and gardener's cottage were in the rear, and there were extensive gardens and a croquet lawn.

The entrance is in the middle of the house and faces east. The high double front doors are of solid walnut, with a semi-circular fanlight. A vestibule with walls panelled in walnut has double doors to the hall surrounded by coloured leaded glass. On the south side of the forty-foot-long hall is a large fireplace with a high, ornately carved walnut mantel and a throne-like seat in each side, carved in one piece with the mantel. Two doors on both right and left walls have wide, flat walnut hoods on console brackets, with a half-lion rampart carved in the keystone of each door. The same lion was on Brown's bookplates and writing paper. The ground floor ceilings are sixteen feet high.

South of the hall is the double drawing room with folding doors. Sunlight pours in from long triple windows in each of the bays, and decorative plasterwork enriches the cornice and ceiling medallions. The walls were covered with silk in a delicate floral pattern. In the back drawing room the wide mantel is of white veined marble, with George and Anne's initials entwined in the centre.

In 1880 a drunken ex-employee of *The Globe* shot George Brown in the leg. At the time the wound did not seem serious. However, it became gangrenous and six weeks later he died, leaving a heartbroken family. Lambton Lodge had been their family home for only a few years.

The murderer was hanged, and in 1882 *The Globe* was bought by Senator Jaffray.

Anne and the three children remained in the house for seven more years. Her daughters Margaret and Catharine had the distinction of being in the first class at the University of Toronto which admitted women. One should note that this small group of intrepid girls were not allowed to sit in classrooms where they could distract the male students! Instead, these "unnatural" women had to sit in an adjoining room where they might or might not hear what the professor was saying. It was a Turkish seraglio in Victorian Toronto, only the girls were not required to wear veils. George's daughters were among five women who received degrees in 1885.

Anne and George Brown. Mrs. Brown is holding her oldest child, Maggie, one of the first women to graduate from the University of Toronto.

— Ontario Archives

Anne rented Lambton Lodge and returned to Scotland. Her children followed. George, the only son, went into his grandfather's publishing firm. All three children married and remained in Scotland.

In 1889 Anne sold Lambton Lodge to Duncan Coulson, General Manager of the Bank of Toronto, for $31,600.

It is said that when George Brown's widow met Sir John A. Macdonald's widow, they did not speak. Both lonely old women returned to Scotland and would have had a great deal in common, but both were loyal to their husbands' old hostilities.

In 1916 Coulson and his wife died. After World War I a training centre was desperately needed for blinded veterans, so in 1919 the Canadian National Institute for the Blind moved to Lambton Lodge, and in the following year the Government bought the house from the

Coulson estate for $50,000. The property was turned over to the C.N.I.B. Captain Edwin Baker was put in charge.

"Eddie" Baker, a blinded officer, was trained by Sir Arthur Pearson at St. Dunstan's in London, England. Pearson's inspiration to blinded soldiers made his name a natural choice for the centre, and Lambton Lodge was henceforth called "Pearson Hall" with the name in large gilt letters on the fanlight above the door.

Captain Baker, M.C., Croix de Guerre, later Colonel, and holder of many honorary degrees, was the guiding spirit of Pearson Hall for thirty-four years, his office being the second-floor room with the black marble mantel. Pearson Hall was both residence and training centre, where thousands of blinded soldiers were rehabilitated. Eddie Baker's magnificent example helped them lead nearly normal lives.

Few changes were made in the house. The former library became the C.N.I.B. library with a walk-in vault and records-room built on the north side. The dining room became the board room. Dances were held in the drawing room and games played on the lawns. The brick stable became a paint shop. When three annexes had to be added, the stained glass window at the stair landing was sacrificed, but the gracious rooms were little changed.

Pearson Hall served magnificently but was outgrown. In 1956 when the C.N.I.B. built new headquarters on Bayview Avenue, Metropolitan Toronto bought Pearson Hall for $200,000 and leased it to the Metropolitan Toronto Association for the Mentally Retarded. The Association spent half a million dollars converting it into a special school. A paved playground and parking lot replaced the trees and lawns.

A firewall was built at the stair landing and another at the top of the third floor stairs. The ornate walnut mantel which projected so far into the front drawing room was removed, a small plain one substituted, and the fireplace partly bricked up. A sprinkler system was installed, and partitions converted the large rooms into offices and classrooms. The name in the fanlight was altered.

Long Garth
1882-1969

The late 1870s and early 1880s were depression years, when few large houses were built in Toronto. The next decade, however, was better, and exclusive Jarvis Street, where the mansions of the wealthy were concentrated, found it had a rival in St. George Street.

In 1882 there were only thirteen houses on the east side of St. George between College and Bloor, and there was not a single street intersecting the east side. Its proximity to the University of Toronto began to attract professors who joined barristers and others already there, and, when the Ontario Parliament Buildings were completed in nearby Queen's Park in 1892, new houses began to spring up on St. George Street.

The road was paved with large bricks and there was a pleasant tree-lined boulevard on each side.

In 1882 Robert Ramsay Wright, a Scottish professor of biology, built and occupied the house at 199. (The new Zoology Building, erected on the campus in 1965, is called the "Ramsay Wright Building.") Since professors have never been wealthy, the early St. George Street homes were not mansions.

In 1889 Byron Edmund Walker, General Manager of the Canadian Bank of Commerce, bought Wright's house and in the same year an official entrance to Queen's Park was opened south of the house. It was merely a lane, and it was closed in 1917.

Walker called his new home "Long Garth," probably because of the long lane next to it, since *garth*, a Saxon word, meant a close, alley, or passage to a property.

Walker was born near Caledonia, Ontario. After a successful career with the Canadian Bank of Commerce, he became its President in 1907 and a recognized authority on finance. In 1874 he married Mary Alexander. They had four sons and three daughters.

Long Garth was a High Victorian house of red bricks, laid in a pleasing pattern. The tall, triple chimneys were linked top and bottom. A handsome wrought-iron fence enclosed the front of the hundred-foot lot and shallow semi-circular drive. There was a private driveway along the north side, but the stables were not on the property. They were on the south side of nearby Sussex Avenue, with coachman's quarters above.

The library contained a row of glass-fronted bookcases, together with cabinets of fitted drawers and cupboards where Walker's collection of prints and etchings was stored. Much of this collection is now in the Art Gallery of Ontario.

In addition to his career as a banker, Byron Walker had other interests. For years he collected fossils, and the gift to the University of his extensive collection and library on palaeontology was the cornerstone of this department in the Royal Ontario Museum. He was an art connoisseur, a discriminating collector of prints, paintings, and porcelain, and he occasionally lectured on art.

He was the founder and first President of the Champlain Society, and in 1898 was President of the Canadian Institute (later the Royal). He was briefly Chairman of the Board of Governors of the University of Toronto and the first Honorary Consul-General of Japan in Toronto.

In 1910 Byron E. Walker was knighted. Henceforth he was known as Sir Edmund Walker.

Sir Edmund's collections had grown so large that in 1908 he doubled the size of the drawing room by adding a one-storey extension to the south side, with pairs of columns at each end of the opening between the old and new parts.

He did not consider that his drawing room was a private art gallery. He was not ostentatious; he bought what he enjoyed, and his collections were part of his home. Long Garth was filled with paintings, Japanese prints, Chinese ceramics, Oriental rugs, and Dutch pottery.

Sir Edmund became first President of the Art Museum of Toronto

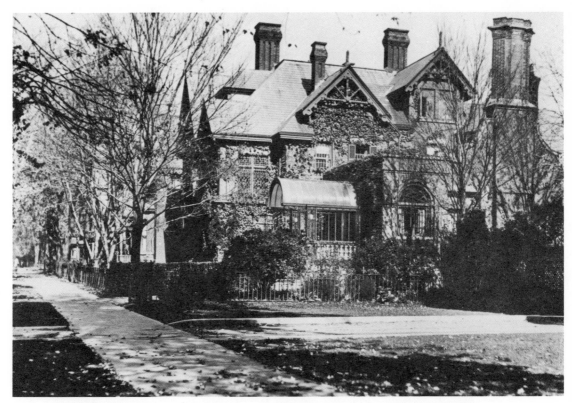

For many years Long Garth was the comfortable home of Sir Edmund Walker, banker and art connoisseur. He was the first President of the Art Museum of Toronto, later the Art Gallery of Ontario.

— Trinity College Archives

which, in turn, became the Art Gallery of Toronto. The present Art Gallery of Ontario, a descendant of these bodies, has a large central court named for Walker in honour of his generous gifts and expert advice.

He was Chairman of the Board of Trustees of the National Gallery in Ottawa from 1909 until his death, serving on the advisory board to purchase paintings.

Since the 1890s he had been urging the founding of a provincial museum. He persuaded Sir James Whitney that the government should join the University in building one. Today a bronze bust in the rotunda of the Royal Ontario Museum commemorates him as one of the founders and the first Chairman of the Board of Trustees.

The library at Long Garth, 99 St. George Street. The cabinets contained Sir Edmund Walker's fine collection of prints and etchings.

— Dr. H.A. Hunter

In 1924 Sir Edmund Walker died at Long Garth, a year after the death of Lady Walker. He had recently been appointed Chancellor of the University of Toronto.

In 1925 Long Garth was sold to Trinity University for $55,000. Trinity had moved from Queen Street to Hoskin Avenue and needed a temporary residence for its women students. The house became the new St. Hilda's College.

In 1969 Long Garth was demolished. Today the site is a parking lot, waiting for the University of Toronto to decide its fate.

The handsome carved mantel from the old dining room and a portrait of Sir Edmund will be used in the proposed Sir Edmund Walker Hall, to commemorate the man who so well served the University of Toronto, the Royal Ontario Museum, and the Art Gallery of Ontario.

Acknowledgments

Much of the information regarding the history of named houses in Toronto would have been impossible to find without the help of various descendants of the original owners. They have been unfailingly gracious and helpful, in both personal interviews and by correspondence. They have been patient with my repeated enquiries, and, in many cases, have been kind enough to loan prized family documents and photographs. Every conversation, whether by telephone or in person, was a pleasure.

I would like to express my gratitude to Mrs. R.M. Bethune, nee Elsie T. Wishart (Bellevue); Mr. Joseph de Pencier (Davenport); Mr. Antony Adamson (Devon House); Mrs. A. Goulding, nee Dorothy Massey (Euclid Hall); Mrs. C. Cambie, nee C. Evelyn Nordheimer, Mrs. P.Kerrin, Major Roy Nordheimer (Glen Edyth); Mr. F.C. Deacon, Mr. Coulter Deacon, Miss Violet Boyd and Mrs. D.J. Fairbrother, nee Kitty Jarvis (Glen Hurst); Mrs. C.B. Lindsey, nee Wanda Gzowski (The Hall); Mrs. H.P. Wright, nee Norah Blake (Holland House, Humewood II); Mr. Verschoyle Blake, Mrs. F.H. Marani, nee Constance Blake (Humewood II); Mr. Patrick Vernon Q.C., Mr. Hugh Vernon, Mrs. R.J. Gardner and Mrs. Henry Nicholls (Homewood); Mrs. Henry Burden and Mrs. Derek Phillips (Humewood III); Mr. Wentworth D. Walker (Long Garth); Miss M. Rozel Pipon (Northfield); Mr. Richard Crampton (Oakham House); Mrs. J.M. Routledge, nee Macdonald and Mrs. F.H. Lytle, nee Macdonald (Oaklands); Mrs. James O'Reilly, nee Marion Meredith (Rosedale); Mrs. H.M. Cawthra-Elliot, nee Grace Cawthra (Yeadon Hall).

In addition to helpful grandsons and granddaughters of early owners of Toronto houses, a number of men and women generously shared their memories of families, neighbourhoods, and particular houses:

Mrs. H.J. Sissons, nee Constance Kerr, Miss Rose Macdonald, Mr. Herbert Staples, and Mr. Frank Yewman (Culloden); Mr. and Mrs. M.F. Feheley (Drumsnab); Mrs. Mona Gould and D.C. Woodiwiss (Humewood III); Miss Irene Moyer, Miss Grace Worts, and Mr. W.F. Clayson (Lambton Lodge); Mr. W.C. Walls (Northfield); Mr. B. Cavan (Oakham House); Mrs. K. Riddell (Pendarvis); Miss M. Rogers (Sherborne Villa); Mrs. J. Wickham-Barnes (Wychwood).

Many librarians and archivists were helpful, but I would especially like to thank Miss Edith Firth and Mrs. Christine Mosser of the Metro Toronto Central Library, Miss Glenna Tishaw, Toronto City Archives, Mrs. E. Marsland, Wellesley Hospital Library, Mr. Henri Pilon, Trinity College Archives, Father Shook, St. Michael's College, and Brother Alban, De La Salle College.

And, finally, I am most grateful to Miss Ellen Russell for her excellent photographs of houses still standing.

Bibliography

Manuscript Collections

BALDWIN PAPERS, Ontario Archives. Metro Toronto Central Library.

BLAKE PAPERS, Ontario Archives.

BOULTON, H.J., PAPERS, Ontario Archives.

CHURCH RECORDS, Ontario Archives. The Anglican, Presbyterian, Roman Catholic, and United Churches maintain their own archives in Toronto. These contain records of Births, Baptisms, Marriages, and Deaths, which are most useful to genealogists. The United Church Archives at Victoria College have Methodist Church Records and some Presbyterian Records.

CROWN LAND PAPERS, YORK TOWNSHIP, Ontario Archives.

ELMSLEY, CAPT. JOHN, LETTER BOOKS 1828-31, Miss Nina Elmsley Collection.

HOWARD, JOHN G., Journals and Correspondence, Metro Toronto Central Library.

HOWARD, JOHN G., Architectural Drawings, Metro Toronto Central Library.

JARVIS-POWELL PAPERS, Ontario Archives.

O'BRIEN (Mrs. George, nee M. Gapper) JOURNALS 1828-38, Ontario Archives.

PATTESON, T.C., PAPERS, Ontario Archives.

PRICE-JACKES, LETTER BOOKS AND PAPERS, Author's possession.

REED, T.A., SCRAPBOOKS, Metro Toronto Central Library. 12 vols. of clippings.

ROBINSON, J.B., PAPERS, Ontario Archives.

RUSSELL, ELIZABETH, Correspondence, Diaries, Metro Toronto Central Library.

RUSSELL, PETER, PAPERS, Ontario Archives.

SIMCOE, (MRS. J.G.), PAPERS, Ontario Archives, Correspondence, Diary, Sketches.

SMITH, LARRATT, DIARY, Metro Toronto Central Library.

STRACHAN, JOHN, LETTER BOOKS, Ontario Archives.

Secondary Sources

Adam, G. Mercer, *Toronto Old and New*, The Mail Publishing Company, Toronto, 1891.

Adamson, Anthony and Willard, John, *The Gaiety of Gables*, McClelland and Stewart Limited, Toronto, 1974.

Alfred, Brother, *Catholic Pioneers in Upper Canada*, Macmillan Company of Canada Limited, Toronto, 1947.

Andre, John, *Infant Toronto*, Centennial Press, Toronto, 1971.

Arthur, Eric, *Toronto, No Mean City*, University of Toronto Press, Toronto, 1964. *The Early Architecture of the Province of Ontario*, The Journal Royal Architectural Institute of Canada, 1927-1928. *The Early Buildings of Ontario*, University of Toronto Press, Toronto, 1938.

Arthur, Eric, *et al.*, *St. Lawrence Hall*, Thomas Nelson and Sons, Don Mills, 1969.

Baldwin, R.M. and J., *The Baldwins and the Great Experiment*, Longmans, Canada, Toronto, 1969.

Baxter Publishing Company, *Toronto and Early Canada*, A Catalogue of the Toronto and Early Canada Picture Collection in the Toronto Public Library, Toronto, 1964.

Baine, R.P. and McMurray, A.L., *Toronto, An Urban Study*, Clarke, Irwin and Company Limited, Toronto, 1970.

Beers, J.H. & Co. (Pub.), *Commemorative Biographical Record of County of York*, Toronto, 1907.

Blake, Verschoyle B. and Greenhill, R., *Rural Ontario*, University of Toronto Press, Toronto, 1969.

Bonis, R.R., *A History of Scarborough*, pub. by Scarborough Public Library, Scarborough, 1965.

Boylen, J.C., *York Township, An Historical Survey*, pub. by Township of York, 1954. *The Story of Castle Frank*, Rous and Mann Press Ltd., Toronto, 1959.

Bremmer, R.M. *Report on City of Toronto Bridges and Under-passes*, Toronto, 1968.

Bruce, Herbert, A., *Varied Operations*, Longmans, Green and Company, Toronto, 1958.

Canniff, William, *The Medical Profession in Upper Canada 1793-1850*, Wm. Briggs, Toronto, 1894.

Careless, J.M.S., *Brown of the Globe*, 2 volumes, Macmillan Company of Canada Limited, Toronto, 1959, 1963.

Cawthra, Henry and Others, *Past and Present, The Cawthra Family*, Privately printed, Ontario Archives, Toronto, 1924.

Chadwick, Edward Marion, *Ontarian Families*, 2 volumes, Ralph, Smith & Co., Toronto, 1894-1898.

Chambers, E.J., *The Queen's Own Rifles of Canada*, E.L. Ruddy, Toronto, 1901. *The Governor-General's Body Guard*, E.L. Ruddy, Toronto, 1902.

Clark, C.S., *Of Toronto the Good, A Social Study*, Toronto Publishing Company, Toronto, 1898.

Corelli, Rae, *The Toronto That Used To Be*, Toronto Star Ltd., Toronto, 1964.

Creighton, Donald, *John A. Macdonald*, 2 volumes, Macmillan Company of Canada Limited, Toronto, 1952, 1955.

Creighton, Louella, *The Elegant Canadians*, McClelland and Stewart Limited, Toronto, 1967.

Cutts, Anson Bailey, *The Old Scottish Architecture of Ontario*, Canadian Geographical Magazine, 1949.

Dau (Ed.), *The Society Blue Book, A Social Directory*, DAU Publishing Company, New York, 1911, 1920.

Davies, Blodwen, *Storied York, Toronto Old and New*, Ryerson Press, Toronto, 1931.

Denison, George, Taylor, *Soldiering in Canada*, G. V. Morang and Co., Toronto, 1900.

Denison, Richard, L., *The Canadian Pioneer Denison Family of County York, England, and County York, Ontario*, 4 volumes (typescript), Toronto, 1952.

de Volpi, Chas., P., *Toronto, A Pictorial Record, 1813-1882*, Dev-Sco Publications Ltd., Montreal, 1965.

Dickson, G. and Adam, G.M., *A History of Upper Canada College 1829-1892*, Rowsell and Hutchison, Toronto, 1893.

Duff, J. Clarence, *Pen Sketches of Historic Toronto*, J. Clarence Duff 2 volumes, J. Clarence Duff, Toronto, 1967- 1972.

Edgar, (Lady) Matilda, *Ten Years in Upper Canada 1805-1815*, William Briggs, Toronto, 1890.

Engelhardt, G.W., *Toronto Its Board of Trade*, George W. Engelhardt, Toronto 1897.

Firth, Edith G. (ed.), *Town of York*, 2 volumes. University of Toronto Press, Toronto, 1962, 1966.

Fligg, E.E. (Pub.), *Toronto Illustrated*, Toronto, 1906.

Fraser, Alexander, *The 48th Highlanders of Toronto*, E.L. Ruddy, Toronto, 1900.

French, William, *A Most Unlikely Village*, Corporation of Village of Forest Hill, 1964.

Gillen, Mollie, *The Masseys*, Ryerson Press, Toronto, 1965.

Glazebrook, G. P. de T., *The Story of Toronto*, University of Toronto Press, Toronto, 1971.

Goad, Charles E., *Atlas of the City of Toronto and Vicinity*, Charles E. Goad, Toronto 1884, 1890, 1910.

Gowans, Alan, *Looking at Architecture in Canada*, Oxford University Press, Toronto, 1958.

Guillet, Edwin C., *Toronto Illustrated From Trading Post to Great City*, Ontario Publishing Company Limited, Toronto, 1934. *Lives and Times of the Patriots*, Ontario Publishing Company Limited, Toronto, 1938.

Hale, Katherine, *Toronto Romance of a Great City*, Cassell & Co. Limited, Toronto, 1956.

Hathaway, E.J., *Jesse Ketchum and His Times*, McClelland and Stewart Limited, Toronto, 1929.

Henderson, Elmes, *Bloor St. Toronto and the Village of Yorkville in 1849,*
Ontario Historical Society Papers and Records Vol. 26, Toronto,
1930.

Hodgins, J.G. (Ed.), *The Establishment of Schools and Colleges in Ontario*
1792-1910, L.K. Cameron, Toronto, 1910.

Hounsom, E.W., *Toronto in 1810,* Ryerson Press, Toronto, 1970.

Howard, John George, *Incidents in the Life of John George Howard of*
Colborne Lodge, Copp, Clark & Company, Toronto, 1885.

Hunter, A.F., *The Probated Wills of Persons Prominent in the Public*
Affairs of Early Upper Canada, Ontario Historical Society Papers and
Records, Vol. 23, 1926, containing Peter Russell's will, 1808,
and Elizabeth Russell's will, 1811. Volume 24, 1927, containing James Macaulay's will, 1821.

Innis, Mary Quayle (ed.), *Mrs. Simcoe's Diary*, Macmillan Company of
Canada Limited, Toronto, 1965.

Jackes, Lyman B., *Tales of North Toronto*, 2 volumes, Canadian Historical Press, Toronto, 1948.

Jameson, Anna, *Winter Studies and Summer Rambles in Canada*,
Saunders and Ogley, London, 1838.

Jarvis, Edward Aemilius, *An Account of the Life of*, (by himself)
Typescript, Privately published, Toronto, 1940.

Jarvis, Julia, *Three Centuries of Robinsons, The Story of a Family*, Published by author, Toronto, 1953.

Jarvis, Mary Hoskin, *Historical Street Names of Toronto,* The Women's
Canadian Historical Society of Toronto, 1933.

Jukes, Mary, *New Life in Old Houses,* Longmans Canada Ltd., Don
Mills 1966.

Kerr, D. and Spelt, J., *The Changing Face of Toronto.* Department of
Mines; Technical Survey. A Study in Urban Geography. Ottawa,
1965.

Kilbourn, William, *The Toronto Book,* Macmillan Company of Canada
Limited, Toronto, 1976.

Langton, John, *Early Days in Upper Canada,* Letters of John Langton
edited by W.A. Langton, Macmillan Company of Canada
Limited, Toronto, 1926.

Lindsey, Charles, *The Life and Times of William Lyon Mackenzie,* 2 volumes, P.R. Randall, Toronto, 1862.

Lizars, Kathleen M., and Robina, *In the Days of the Canada Company*, William Briggs, Toronto, 1896.

Lorimer, James, *The Ex,* James Lewis and Samuel, Toronto, 1973.

Macmurchy, Angus, and Reed, T.A., *Our Royal Town of York*, Angus Macmurchy and T.A. Reed, Toronto, 1929.

Macnab, J.E., *Toronto's Industrial Growth to 1891*, Ontario Historical Society, Ontario History, 1955.

Macrae, Marion, and Adamson, Anthony, *The Ancestral Roof*, Clarke, Irwin and Company Limited, Toronto, 1963.

McLeod and Allan (Pub.), *One Hundred Glimpses of Toronto*, Toronto, 1901.

Massey, Raymond, *When I Was Young*, McClelland and Stewart Limited, Toronto, 1976.

Masters, D.C., *The Rise of Toronto 1850-1890*, University of Toronto Press, Toronto, 1947.

Meredith, Alden G., *Mary's Rosedale and Gossip of Little York*, Graphic Publishers Ltd., Ottawa, 1928.

Mickle, Sara, *Colborne Lodge. The Owner of Colborne Lodge*, The Women's Canadian Historical Society of Toronto, 1927.

Middleton, Jesse Edgar, *Municipality of Toronto*, 3 volumes, Dominion Publishing Company of Canada, Toronto, 1923. *Toronto's One Hundred Years 1834-1934*, Centennial Committee, Toronto, 1934.

Mika, Nick, and Helma, *Toronto Magnificent City*, Mika Silk Screening Limited, Belleville.

Miles and Company, (pub.), *Illustrated Historical Atlas, County of York*, Toronto, 1878.

Mitchell, John, *The Settlement of York County*, Corporation County of York, County of York, 1950.

Morgan, Henry J. (ed.), *Canadian Men and Women of the Time*, William Briggs, Toronto, 1862, 1898, 1912. *Types of Canadian Women*, William Briggs, Toronto, 1903.

Mulvaney, C. Pelham, *Toronto Past and Present*, W. E. Calger, Toronto, 1884.

Neelands, E.V., *Old Toronto Streets and Landmarks*, The Women's Canadian Historical Society of Toronto, 1920.

Paterson, Gilbert C., *Land Settlement in Upper Canada*, Department of Archives Ontario, Toronto, 1920.

Pearson, W.H., *Recollections and Records of Toronto of Old*, William Briggs, Toronto, 1914.

Pierce, Lorne, *The House of Ryerson 1829-1954*, Toronto, 1954.

Plaunt, Dorothy R., "The Hon. Peter Russell, Administrator of Upper Canada 1796-99," Canadian Hist. Review, Vol. XX, 1939.

Poulton, Ron, *The Paper Tyrant, John Ross Robertson*, Clarke, Irwin and Company, Toronto, 1971.

Read, D.B., *Lives of the Judges*, Rowsell and Hutchison, Toronto, 1888. *Life and Times of General John Graves Simcoe*, George Virtue pub., Toronto, 1890. *Lives of the Lieutenant-Governors of Upper Canada and Ontario 1792-1899*, William Briggs, Toronto, 1900.

Reed, T.A., "Toronto's Early Architects," Journal Royal Architectural Institute of Canada, February, 1950.

Reed, T.A., *Historical Value of Street Names*, Ontario Historical Society Papers and Records, Volume 25, 1929.

Rempel, John, *Building with Wood*, University of Toronto Press, Toronto, 1967.

Richmond, John, and West, Bruce, *Around Toronto*, Doubleday Canada Limited, Toronto, 1969.

Riddell, William Renwick, *The Legal Profession in Upper Canada*, Law Society of Upper Canada, Toronto, 1916. *The Life and Times of William Dummer Powell*, Historical Commission 1924, Lansing, Michigan. *The Life of John Graves Simcoe*, McClelland and Stewart Limited, Toronto, 1926. *The First Attorney-General of Upper Canada*, John White O.H.S. Papers and V. 23, Records, 1926.

Ritchie, T. *et al.*, *Canada Builds*, University of Toronto Press, Toronto, 1967.

Roaf, James R., *Some Recollections of Davenport Road in the early 60's. Residences in or Near Yorkville.* (typescript), Toronto, 1935.

Robertson, John Ross (Comp.), *Landmarks of Toronto*, 6 volumes, Toronto, 1894-1914. Originally appeared in columns in *The Evening Telegram*. Published by *Toronto Telegram*. *What Art Has Done for Canadian History*, A Guide to the J.R. Robertson Historical Collection, Toronto, 1917.

Robertson, John Ross (Ed.), *The Diary of Mrs. Simcoe*, The Ontario Publishing Company Limited, Toronto, 1934.

Robinson, C.B. (Pub.), *History of Toronto and County of York, Ontario*, 2 volumes, Toronto, 1885.

Robinson, (Sir) C.W., *Life of Sir John Beverley Robinson*, Morang and Company Limited, Toronto, 1904.

Robinson, Percy, *Toronto during the French Regime 1615-1793*. Ryerson Press, Toronto, 1933.

Russell, Peter, Correspondence edited by E.A. Cruikshank, 3 vols. Toronto 1932-36. Ontario Historical Society.

Scadding, Henry, *Toronto of Old Collections and Recollections*, Adam, Stevenson and Company, Toronto, 1873.

Scadding, H. and Dent, J.C. *Toronto Past and Present*, Historical and Descriptive, Hunter, Rose and Company, Toronto, 1884.

Schull, J., *One Hundred Years of Banking in Canada*, Copp, Clark Publishing Co. Ltd., Toronto, 1956.

Simcoe, J.G., Correspondence, edited by E.A. Cruikshank, 5 vols. Ontario Historical Society, Toronto, 1923-30.

Sissons, Charles B., *History of Victoria College*, University of Toronto Press, Toronto, 1952.

Smith, Elspeth (Comp.), *Recording Toronto,* A Catalogue of early buildings in the Town of York and City of Toronto from the Picture Collection of the Toronto Public Library, Toronto, 1960.

Spendlove, F. St. G., *The Face of Early Canada*, Ryerson Press, Toronto, 1958.

Spragge, George W. (Ed.), *The John Strachan Letter Book.1812-1834*, The Ontario Historical Society Papers and Records, Toronto, 1946.

Taylor, C.C., *Toronto Called Back from 1892-1847*, William Briggs, Toronto, 1892.

Thomas, Clara, *Love and Work Enough, The Life of Anna Jameson*, University of Toronto Press, Toronto, 1967.

Thompson, Austin Seton, *Spadina, A Story of Old Toronto*, Pagurian Press Limited, Toronto, 1975.

Toronto Civic Historical Committee (Pub.), *Historic Toronto*, Toronto, 1953.

Toronto Directories, 1837, 1846, 1856, 1859, 1861, then annually.

Toronto Scrap Book, 12 vols. Toronto Public Library, City Hall Branch.

University of Toronto (Pub.), *The University of Toronto and Its Colleges 1827-1906*, University Library, Toronto, 1906.

Walker, Frank N., *Sketches of Old Toronto*, Longmans Canada Limited, Don Mills, 1965.

Wallace, W. Stewart, *A History of the University of Toronto 1827-1927*, University of Toronto Press, Toronto, 1927. *The Dictionary of Canadian Biography*, 2 volumes, Macmillan Company of Canada Limited, Toronto, 1945.

West, Bruce, *Toronto*, Doubleday and Company, New York, 1967.

Wilson, G.E., *The Life of Robert Baldwin*, Ryerson Press, Toronto, 1933.

Yeigh, Frank, *Ontario's Parliament Buildings 1792-1892*, The Williamson Book Company, Toronto, 1893.

York Directories, 1815, 1833.

Index